THE CHANGING SCHOOL CURRICULUM

THE CHANGING SCHOOL CURRICULUM

by **JOHN I. GOODLAD**

*University of California, Los Angeles, and
Institute for Development of Educational Activities*

with **RENATA VON STOEPHASIUS**

Ford Foundation, New York

and **M. FRANCES KLEIN**

University of California, Los Angeles

To Howard E. Wilson

August, 1966
Library of Congress Catalog Card Number 66-23975
Additional copies of this report are available
without cost from the offices of
The Fund for the Advancement of Education,
477 Madison Avenue, New York, New York 10022.

THE FUND FOR THE ADVANCEMENT OF EDUCATION is a philanthropic organization established in 1951 by the Ford Foundation to work in the field of formal education. Its chief activity is the support of experimental programs that hold promise of advancing education in American schools and colleges. To date the Fund has been granted approximately $70 million by the Ford Foundation.

Design: Gene Paul Muzio
Printing: The Georgian Press, Inc.

CONTENTS

PREFACE

The curricula of our schools and colleges have always been in a process of change, but the change usually has not been fundamental. New content was added; some old material was discarded. Sometimes whole courses disappeared and were replaced. But more often than not, the new courses looked much like their predecessors. The gradual process of curriculum change tended to reflect the relatively gradual evolution of society itself.

At the end of World War II, however, the schools in the United States were ready for more sweeping changes. The country had passed through some twenty years of economic depression and war; we had lost sight of education as a potent force for societal welfare, and had neglected our schools. The near absence of scientific and mathematical comprehension among school graduates, revealed by the wartime testing programs, showed that something was wrong with our educational institutions. It was an alarming situation, the more so as this nation and the world were standing at the threshold of an era of unprecedented scientific development in which education would have to play a significant role. Educators, parents, and other interested citizens voiced their concern and thus were instrumental in starting what has proved to be a substantial reform in the curricula of our elementary and secondary schools.

One of the characteristics of this reform movement is that it is discipline centered rather than child or society centered. That is, the emphasis is on updating and reorganizing those academic disciplines that are considered basic in the pre-collegiate curriculum. Beginning with mathematics, the physical and biological sciences, and foreign languages, reform has now spread to the social sciences and, to a lesser degree, to the humanities, the arts, and health education.

By 1963 the movement was a dozen years old, although it had been significantly robust for only half of them. In that year Alvin C. Eurich, then Vice President of the Fund for the Advancement of Education, asked me to examine and to report on the new curriculum projects, to describe them, to assess their advantages and disadvantages, and to suggest directions for the future. My report, *School Curriculum Reform in the United States,* was published by the Fund in 1964. In that effort I was ably assisted by George Temp, now with the Educational Testing Service in Princeton, New Jersey.

The present report is the result of a continued analysis of curriculum materials prepared by a fast-growing number of projects committed to improving the subjects taught in our schools. As before, data and impressions were gathered through correspondence and interviews with the directors of the projects, by visiting schools that were testing or examining these newer materials, by reading progress reports, and by studying critiques prepared by others.

The overview presented in Section I is intended to provide a summary of the shaping forces, the characteristic features, and what the writer considers to be the major strengths and weaknesses of the current curriculum reform. Section II describes most of the major projects. Section III discusses some of the problems and issues that arise in this and, in fact, in virtually all curriculum developments. Section IV attempts to place these problems and issues within a larger context. Although some material is drawn directly from the 1964 report, this is essentially a new description and critique.

For the work of my associates, Renata von Stoephasius and Frances Klein, I am most appreciative. I alone, however, assume full responsibility for what appears in print. I am grateful to Marion Braun, Arline Duff, Ann Edwards, Domenica Fitzgerald, and Corann Pesquira for their assistance in preparing the manuscript for production. I wish to express my gratitude also to the Fund for the Advancement of Education for publishing and distributing this report.   J. I. G.

OVERVIEW

Many educational changes have been proposed and some have been effected since the early 1950's but to describe what has been happening to the schools as "revolutionary" would be overstating the case. The talk far exceeds the achievement. Nevertheless, many of our schools differ markedly from what they were even a decade ago. Greatly significant changes have occurred in the curriculum and a massive reformulation of what is to be taught and learned in our schools is under way.

It has been said that Sputnik (1957) put subject matter back into the curriculum. This is an overstatement in at least two respects. First, subject matter was never out of the curriculum; there could not be a curriculum without it. However, much of what was taught in elementary and secondary schools in 1950 was sterile and out of date. Layers of minor revisions had been pasted upon previous layers of minor revisions until school subjects had lost much of the coherence and identity they once possessed. Complete rethinking was called for. Second, concern for a more discipline-centered curriculum goes back much further than 1957. The work of the University of Illinois Committee on School Mathematics, for example, began in 1951. Nonetheless, the launching of the first Russian satellite must be acknowledged as a direct cause of vastly accelerated curriculum revision, notably in mathematics and the physical sciences.

The beginnings of the current curriculum reform movement, now well along in its second decade, were clearly evident in the years immediately following World War II. The recruitment of young men for the armed services had revealed shocking inadequacies in the science and mathematics backgrounds of high-school graduates. They were due partly to the limited quantity of work in these fields and partly to the quality of the teaching. As scientists became increasingly aware of this situation, some of them began to sense their responsibility toward the problem. Their subsequent involvement in pre-collegiate curriculum reform has been both a factor producing change and a significant characteristic of the movement.

But curriculum reform probably would have evolved much more slowly and quietly had there not been a number of other contributing causes. The anticipated postwar economic collapse, predicted frequently and gloomily, did not materialize. An expanding, prosperous middle class of ambitious young men and women saw education as the means to even better things for their children. They turned to their schools—often new schools in new communities, with young teachers and young administrators—with great expectations. These educators responded, reaching out eagerly to become co-workers in the trial use of materials prepared or backed by illustrious scholars in prestigious universities, an association that was not lost on college-conscious parents. The first round of school curriculum reform, then, was a middle-class and upper-middle-class affair, embracing primarily the college-bound students. The cry of the disadvantaged was as yet only a whisper.

While new communities were springing up, old values were crumbling. Job opportunities took young couples away from familiar haunts to challenges they had not faced before. A new kind of unemployment appeared: unemployment in the midst of plenty because of job obsolescence. Very little was "for sure." People were beginning to realize that a fast-changing culture demanded both adaptability and a rational approach to new problems. The old ways of keeping school would not suffice, either.

Meanwhile, knowledge was piling up at an intimidating rate. But sheer accumulation presented only part of the problem. All knowledge is subject to revision following new insights into the nature of phenomena. A fact is a fact from some but not all perspectives—and then often only temporarily. This notion is profoundly stimulating to some people but devastatingly upsetting to others. To cope with the explosion of knowledge, the curriculum needed fresh infusions of content and a comprehensive reorganization.

Federal leadership in Washington has viewed the rapid advances in mathematics, science, and foreign-language teaching as essential to the nation's ultimate strength and status in world affairs. The National Science Foundation has become the primary grantor of funds for school projects in these fields. In the articulation and implementation of President Lyndon B. Johnson's plans for the Great Society, the U.S. Office of Education has greatly expanded the scope of its grants. There has been a rapid shift in the individual and/or society emphasis toward developing the individual for his own as well as for the nation's sake. Increased support for the arts and humanities has followed. Private foundations have been involved in the curriculum reform movement from the beginning; the Ford Foundation quite early recognized this need and supported artistic and humanistic endeavors in and out of the schools.

In effect, then, the more recent and continuing effort for curriculum change in elementary and secondary schools has received its momentum from forces and interests lying largely outside the state and local school systems charged legally with responsibility for determining what to teach.[1] The pervasive nature of these forces and interests as well as their financial support make it easy to see why this movement frequently is labeled "national" and why it is accompanied by the fear of a national curriculum. It is, indeed, nationally influenced, but it is not nationally or federally controlled. The total curriculum has been influenced by federal government sources in that funds have been made available more generously for some subjects than for others, resulting in a curricular imbalance. But federal grantors have been careful to maintain a "hands off" policy when it comes to the production of learning materials. Curriculum makers have been and are free to follow their predilections and are producing curricular alternatives at a bewildering rate. If there are similarities in approach from project to project, they are the consequences of imitation and lack of imagination rather than the imposition of restrictions by funding agencies.

---

1. See John I. Goodlad, "The Curriculum," *The Changing American School,* pp. 32-58. The Sixty-Fifth Yearbook of the National Society for the Study of Education. Chicago: University of Chicago Press, 1966.

Current curriculum reform is described better as nationwide than as national in character. And a new alphabet soup of curriculum projects —BSCS, CBA, ESS, PSSC, SMSG—is becoming part of the diet of American children and youth in school. From the beginning this movement has been directed at teachers and students in the classroom. It has not sought to change the basic structure of American education or the thinking of administrators, although the present curriculum reform wave has profound implications for both. Thousands of teachers have attended year-long or summer institutes designed to update their understanding and teaching of academic disciplines. Millions of children and youths are bringing home assignments in mathematics, for example, that are incomprehensible to their parents. High-school students approach biology, chemistry, and physics in ways and with assumptions that appear different from our own experiences as we recall them. The degree and kind of change varies from subject to subject, from school system to school system, and even from school to school within a single system. Although the movement is nationwide, it is by no means national in the sense of being uniformly prescribed from state to state or from school district to school district.

In virtually every field the focal point for teachers and students alike is an instructional materials package: invariably a textbook or series of textbooks (often paperback) and frequently supplementary books, workbooks, teachers' manuals, film strips, films, programed materials, and laboratory experiments. Students often learn about subject matter through audio-visual media of instruction and whenever possible by directly observing phenomena and the methods of dealing with these phenomena.

There are lessons here for anyone seeking to influence American education,[2] and there are complex issues pertaining to what is to be learned in the schools, who is to determine what is to be learned, and how continuing curriculum revision is to be conducted and controlled.

If previous eras of curriculum development can be described as child centered or society centered, this one can be designated as subject or

2. A 1962 report listed textbooks as the prime determinant of what students study in school. See *The Principals Look at the Schools*, p. 23. The Project on the Instructional Program of the Public Schools. Washington: National Education Association, 1962.

discipline centered. The ends and means of schooling are derived from organized bodies of knowledge. Further, the curriculum is planned by physicists, mathematicians, and historians, and students are encouraged to think like these scholars. The word "structure" has replaced "the whole child" in curriculum jargon.[3]

Many curriculum builders seek to organize their fields around the primary structural elements of each discipline: the concepts, key ideas, principles, and modes of inquiry. It is assumed that understanding these elements (rather than merely possessing the facts) gives the student the intellectual power to attack unfamiliar problems and enables him to grasp intuitively the relationship of new phenomena not previously encountered to phenomena already experienced. Ability to think inductively becomes a built-in goal, and teachers are encouraged to let students discover meanings for themselves.

The current curriculum reform movement is marked by an updating of content, a reorganization of subject matter, and some fresh approaches to methodology in fields traditionally taught in the schools. It is not simply a return to the Three R's. Nor is it a rejection of John Dewey and progressive education. Quite the contrary, on both counts.

But Grandpa would never recognize today's Three R's. And many of the central concerns of progressive education—emphasis on principles rather than facts, on learning through problem solving rather than by precept, and on individual differences, for example—are stressed and extended by some of today's curriculum builders. But the stress, until recently, has been almost exclusively on the discipline as a separate entity in the curriculum: not science but biology, chemistry, or physics; not social studies but history, geography, or economics; not English but literature, composition, or grammar.

The separate-subject approach creates few immediately apparent problems for the secondary school. Traditionally, high-school teachers have been prepared in a major field and supporting disciplines. Teaching that field in the high school permits a smooth transition from their own studies. Fusing two or more subjects, on the other hand, adds a curriculum-planning burden to teaching demands and often calls for

3. See *The Structure of Knowledge and the Curriculum* (edited by G. W. Ford and Lawrence Pugno). Chicago: Rand McNally and Co., 1964.

collaborative effort with colleagues. Perhaps this is why curriculum innovations such as the core curriculum (usually combining English and social studies) never achieved more than very modest success.

But teaching each field as a discrete entity raises some questions about whether the subject matter is meaningful to the adolescent or whether his school day and the rest of his life remain worlds apart. From a more academic point of view, one wonders too about the subjects left out of the curriculum, simply for lack of time. Some fields of study are now more deeply entrenched in the high school than ever before, mostly because large sums of money have been available for their updating. As a consequence, some relatively new subjects representing exciting advances in human knowledge have been left at the curricular periphery —and will remain there unless a deliberate effort is made to include them in the curriculum design. It would seem that there are decisions of curriculum planning whose consequences are too far reaching to be left to subject-matter specialists alone.

The separate-subject approach would create some immediately apparent problems for the elementary school, however. First, in all but a few states, teachers are prepared as generalists rather than as specialists in subject fields. Second, there is a limit to the number of disciplines that can be taught within the time available, and some difficult choices must therefore be made. There simply is no room in the curriculum for thirty or more separate subjects. Third, if the basic structures and concepts of the academic disciplines form the curriculum design of secondary education, what is to be the approach for elementary education? Is there something of a more basic nature than what has been conceived for the high school?

Problems such as these have caused curriculum planners to wonder whether it is wise to build the curriculum revision at the elementary-school level on assumptions that were valid for the secondary school. Some re-examination was called for and new ideas are beginning to emerge. For example, although four major efforts to reorganize the elementary-school science curriculum differ markedly in their emphases, not one of them is committed to developing each science field separately. All see the need either to combine the disciplines at the outset or to begin separately but then to effect syntheses and integrations. The prevailing mood is one of experimentation, of trying a variety of approaches to see what will happen.

The first wave of the current curriculum reform was initiated at the secondary-school level and has refined some initial assumptions. The second wave, just beginning, focuses on the elementary school and is more experimental in character; it questions the earlier assumptions, and in all probability will initiate a fresh round of curriculum revision for the high school.

It must be remembered that the impetus, planning, and financial support for the type of subject-centered curriculum revision now taking place do not come from the state and local school districts legally responsible for pre-collegiate public education in the United States. The curriculum products of the Physical Science Study Committee, the School Mathematics Study Group, the Chemical Bond Approach Project, etc., provide both ends and means of schooling for the classroom. It would be reassuring to believe that school districts use the products of one curriculum study group in preference to another because they have carefully examined them and found them better suited to those aims of education to which the districts are committed. But this is rarely the case. Few state departments of education and even fewer school districts have seriously tried to determine the precise purpose of their schools and the objectives to be achieved. And yet Americans cling stubbornly to the idea of local control of education while permitting, through sheer neglect, many of the most important decisions to be made by remote curriculum planners. To develop an increased awareness of what these decisions are and to whom we are leaving the responsibility for making them is a curricular agenda item for tomorrow.

Another agenda item concerns the problem of fitting the various curricular pieces together. The curriculum and the students of tomorrow may be better served by subjects and subject combinations other than those deemed important today. But curriculum planning takes place in such a piecemeal fashion that across-the-board examination of the total school experience of children and youth is not likely to occur. In all probability, new accretions and formulations will occur in the traditional school subjects if the curriculum revision procedures of the past decade continue. But ongoing inquiry in fields not now firmly established in the curriculum is likely to go unnoticed unless we concentrate on the aims of schooling rather than on the organization of specific subjects.

A third item for tomorrow's agenda pertains to curriculum experimentation. Since local school offices are directly responsible to local patrons and taxpayers they either cannot experiment or do not consider themselves free to do so; and state educational leaders generally do not control or have access to schools that might be used for experimental purposes. Approaches to change, therefore, are almost necessarily cautious; and changes instituted are "safe." Such innovations as are introduced, furthermore, are given an aura of success, achieved most often through an association with a prestigious institution of higher learning. "Experiments" are rarely experiments but are rather the trial-and-error refinement of assumptions that are seldom questioned.

What is needed then to bring a second wave of curriculum reform to a successful conclusion is: 1) a much more precise delineation of local, state, and federal responsibilities for curriculum planning; 2) more curriculum study centers engaged in planning curriculum designs for the whole length and breadth of pre-collegiate education; 3) a number of truly experimental schools in every state.

It is appropriate that the federal government, through the U.S. Office of Education, be engaged in a continuing survey to see which areas of legitimate educational concern are being attended to and which are being neglected. The USOE must maintain whatever assessment and data collecting procedures are essential to such an appraisal function. And Congress, it would seem, must vote the funds necessary for the correction of inequities and shortcomings. It is appropriate, further, for the President of the United States, through his offices, to alert us to our nationwide or regional inadequacies and to stimulate discourse and action. But no state or local government has to concur with the findings or accept funds to correct the shortcomings.

States and local school districts, on the other hand, must make educational commitments and support these commitments with funds. At present, there is no rational basis for separating the curricular responsibilities of these units. City, county, and state education agencies duplicate each other in outrageous fashion. Few states or local districts have clearly formulated statements of educational aims or school functions that are of use in making strategic curricular decisions. Either the state departments of education must establish procedures for making such decisions rationally, or new mechanisms for doing so must be created.

The task of developing and testing curriculum designs from nursery school through high school is probably too large and expensive to be assumed by the states since the combined support of private foundations and the federal government, primarily through the National Science Foundation, was needed merely to revise the curriculum in single academic disciplines. To study, reorganize, and simulate an entire curriculum of subjects and subject combinations not even thought of at present is an infinitely larger and more complex undertaking. It seems reasonable to assume, therefore, that broadly based curriculum centers will be created by federal funds but operated by private, regional, and state agencies.

Tomorrow's curriculum reform also will need schools that enjoy the same freedom of research as do university-affiliated hospitals which serve as laboratories for medical inquiry. These schools will serve as laboratories for educational and curricular inquiry. Attendance at these institutions must be voluntary, i.e., the decision to send a child to an experimental school must rest with the parents, and the decision to admit the child with the professional staff. Only then do the requisite conditions for experimentation exist.

True experimentation presupposes an availability of alternatives to be tested and compared. The creation of a kaleidoscopic range of viable curricular choices and their careful examination are priorities for tomorrow. Let us turn now to descriptions of some alternatives already at hand, alternatives that must be regarded as transitional at best.

ILLUSTRATIVE PROJECTS

During the 1950's, pre-collegiate curriculum reform in the academic disciplines was concerned almost entirely with mathematics and the physical and biological sciences. The scientific emphasis increased markedly in 1957 and has remained strong up to the present. The national interest has been perceived to lie here; with it has come the financial support.

The school curriculum by 1962 was seen by many to be approaching an imbalance. And two years later the writer was still unable to identify and report curriculum rejuvenation of a substantial sort in the social sciences, English, and the arts.[4] By 1966 the social sciences were at the stage the natural sciences had been nearly a decade before. What direction school curricula in these fields will take is still not clear, nor is it clear in the arts and humanities where activity is just beginning.

Curriculum reform in general is proceeding at such a pace that what seems current today is outdated tomorrow. "Old" projects are undergoing drastic revisions; new projects are springing up almost daily. Subsequent descriptions, therefore, had to be limited to a sampling of projects as they existed in June, 1966. Hopefully, however, they suffice to give even the layman a flavor of the new curriculum that is being prepared for our schools.

---

4. *School Curriculum Reform in the United States*. New York: The Fund for the Advancement of Education, 1964.

Mathematics

Fundamental revision of the mathematics curriculum is now well into its second decade. As pointed out in Section I, the reform movement began with mathematics, the work of the University of Illinois Committee on School Mathematics (UICSM) constituting the first project of its kind. Most of the other projects started in 1957 or later.

Mathematics extends from kindergarten through high school, thus accompanying all children and youth for most of their school careers. For this reason, and because curriculum builders in this field were the first to struggle with the problems and issues of revision, mathematics is accorded the most detailed treatment. The seven projects described here illustrate some of the problems common to curricular work in mathematics as well as in other subjects. The question, for example, of whether to encourage the verbalization of a concept when the student first understands its relevance seems to be a recurring problem.

Mathematics, more than any other field, seems to elicit the question, also raised frequently by parents, of whether the newer content and methods are of sufficient immediate practicality. Mathematicians in turn wonder whether the schools and their teachers are providing enough learning opportunities marked by true mathematical inquiry.

The work of the School Mathematics Study Group is sensitive to this issue as it enters another round of revision. E. G. Begle, project director, has issued a nationwide invitation for comments on the teaching of mathematics.[5] The emerging debate is being carried on by parents and teachers who believe that much of what is being taught under the "new" label will be needed only by students who want to become professional mathematicians. Other interested persons attack the new mathematics curriculum as being overly cautious, claiming that current reforms consist of ideas that are more than a century old. Some say the changes have gone too far; others say the changes have not gone far enough.

---

5. New York *Times,* February 20, 1966.

School Mathematics Study Group

The materials of the School Mathematics Study Group are probably the best known and most widely used of all the "new mathematics" programs. The SMSG grew out of a two-day conference sponsored by the American Mathematical Society in February, 1958, and was founded primarily to develop new courses, teaching materials, and methods in the field of mathematics. The Study Group's efforts have been financed by the National Science Foundation at a cost of approximately $8 million.

As an illustration of the kind of mathematics curriculum it considers appropriate and feasible for today's youth, SMSG has prepared sample textbooks for grades K-12. Texts usually appear in a preliminary and a revised form; revised editions are available at present from the Yale University Press but will cease to be published as soon as enough textbooks incorporating the substance of the SMSG materials become commercially available. Supplementary materials prepared by the group include the "New Mathematical Library" for students, and "Studies in Mathematics" for teachers.

Although no official point of view regarding mathematics and its teaching pervades the work of the School Mathematics Study Group, E. G. Begle assumes (and poses the hypothesis) that concepts and their relationships—the structure of mathematics—are central to all mathematics teaching. SMSG courses are characterized by the treatment of relatively conventional topics rather than by the introduction of new topics. Although students manipulate numbers, the prime objective is to develop awareness of the basic properties of mathematics. Students are encouraged to move to progressively higher levels of abstraction.

Textbooks for grades 7 and 8 are designed to develop a sound, intuitive basis for the algebra and geometry courses of grades 9 and 10. These two junior high-school texts emphasize the structure of arithmetic from an algebraic viewpoint, discuss the number system as a progressing development, include metric and non-metric relationships in geometry, and introduce the student to measurement and elementary statistics. The materials for grades 7 and 8 reveal elements of the entire junior and senior high-school sequence: abstract concepts, the role of definition,

23

the development of precise vocabulary and thought, experimentation, and mathematical truth.

The textbooks for grades 10, 11 and 12 do not differ markedly in content from traditional texts but the organization and method of presenting topics are different. For example, *The First Course in Algebra* (for grade 9) emphasizes number behavior rather than the solving of algebraic equations. The course for grade 10 is predominantly plane geometry, but there is some material on solid geometry and an introduction to analytic geometry. Algebra is reviewed at appropriate points. *Intermediate Mathematics* for grade 11 has chapters on trigonometry, vectors, logarithms, mathematical induction, and complex numbers, encouraging a relatively high level of mathematical awareness.

The first book for grade 12 takes students into a study of elementary functions such as the polynomial, exponential, logarithmic, and trigonometric functions, with emphasis on practical applications wherever possible. There is an introduction of simple but geometrically meaningful methods for handling areas, tangents, and maximum-minimum problems that would provide a student with a good intuitive background for a later course in calculus. The second book for grade 12 is an introduction to matrix algebra, formerly reserved for college, and includes applications to solutions of systems of linear equations and to geometry. There is careful attention to algebraic structure. This text is designed to bring the students to the frontiers of mathematics and to provide examples of mathematical patterns that arise in the most varied physical circumstances.

SMSG is currently working on a revision of its secondary-school materials in an effort to prepare a truly integrated, sequential mathematics program for grades 7-12. The revised curriculum will stress the relationship between mathematics and the sciences and will include the equivalent of a full year of calculus, together with some of the basic notions of probability and numerical analysis.

The elementary-school texts, too, will undergo some revisions in order to create an integrated sequence from grade K-6. As presently constituted, grade 4 begins with the concept of sets, and moves to enumeration, including non-decimal base, fractional numbers, multiplication and division of whole numbers, sets of points, recognition of common geometric figures, and linear measurement. Grade 5 deals with factors, primes, common denominators, side and angle relationships of triangles, measurements of angles and area, in addition to the common topics of adding, subtracting, multiplying, and dividing decimal numbers, including decimal fractions. Topics in grade 6 cover integers, whole numbers and their negatives, exponents, multiplication and division of fractional numbers, coordinates, ratios, graphs, central tendency, sets, circles, and volume.

The SMSG approach emphasizes that the concepts of mathematics are part of the whole of mathematics and not unique to any subdivision of the field, such as geometry or algebra. Although a primary objective is the development by the student of a "feeling" for mathematical structure, there is ample opportunity for practicing the conventional skills of computation. The courses are organized into units, each unit presenting topics and problems in mathematical analysis and requiring several weeks for completion. Topics reappear in the sequence, each subsequent appearance calling for deeper treatment and for a thorough review of the topics presented earlier.

The familiarity of many of these topics to experienced teachers explains in part why the SMSG textbooks are so widely used. Perhaps more important, these materials can be used by teachers who have had little or no special preparation for their use other than that provided in the teaching manuals. Being somewhat less specific in its approach to pedagogy than other programs, SMSG does not advocate that verbalization be withheld or that operational and verbal components be systematically related.

Several sub-projects have accompanied SMSG's central task of preparing textbooks and teachers' manuals. A series of thirty half-hour films constitutes an in-service course for elementary-school teachers who want to improve their mathematical knowledge. Texts for junior and senior high-school students have been translated into Spanish and are being used in Puerto Rico. Other special curricula include textbooks for the slower junior high-school student, and a programed version of the *First Course in Algebra*. The Small Publications Project has issued enrichment materials for use by the more capable student. A five-year National Longitudinal Study of Mathematical Achievement is nearing its end; its results are expected to give some indication of what the SMSG program is achieving and of the type of student who profits most and least by it.

As E. G. Begle sees it, the total effort is only beginning to touch on the many curricular and pedagogical issues to be resolved in the long-term improvement of pre-collegiate mathematics. With the task of creating sample curricula for grades K-12 largely finished, SMSG now plans to concentrate on three major concerns: to provide a closer connection between mathematics and the various areas in which mathematics is used; to continue research on how students learn mathematics; and to devise curriculum materials that are suitable for students whose achievement in mathematics is below average.

Greater Cleveland Mathematics Program

The Greater Cleveland Mathematics Program, sponsored by the Educational Research Council of Greater Cleveland, was organized in 1959 to develop a planned and sequential thirteen-year program that is mathematically correct as well as pedagogically sound.

Pupil and teacher materials, published by Science Research Associates, Inc., in Chicago, are now available for grades K-6 and enjoy rather wide use. The curriculum has been planned from the lower grades upward, with "guided discovery" as an essential ingredient. It has been designed to help the student achieve a clear understanding of the structural interrelationship of numbers so that he can eventually apply numbers to problem situations.

Course content for the intermediate grades (4, 5, and 6) has been arranged in a series of twelve books to facilitate pacing for individual classes. Most students require from three to four years to complete the series. Individual learning differences have been compensated for to some degree by varying the learning pace rather than the assignments.

The teachers' guides contain statements of objectives, mathematical background information, procedures for working with children, children's worksheets keyed for the right answers, and suggested evaluation activities. Objectives are stated for each unit of work, usually in terms of student behavior, and provide a reference for the selection of learning opportunities so far as content is concerned. Learning opportunities are organized in a spiraling sequential fashion; topics continually reappear and gradually increase in complexity.

The council's testing and evaluation department supervises the program's evaluation plans. A traveling field force and summer workshops assist cooperating teachers in thirty-one affiliated school districts in the use of the new text. Materials available to the public include two publications, *Key Topics in Mathematics for the Primary Teacher, Key Topics in Mathematics for the Intermediate Teacher,* and six films.

The Madison Project of
Syracuse University and Webster College

The Madison project began in 1957 under the sponsorship of the mathematics department of Syracuse University. (It takes its name from the Madison School in Syracuse, New York, where some department members were then teaching.) Original financial support came from the Marcel Holzer and Alfred P. Sloan foundations, and most of the early work was with culturally deprived children who were doing poorly in school. Encouraged by the results of their work with these children, project members in 1959 began to concentrate their efforts on children with more than average ability who were living in "over-privileged" homes in suburban communities. A second project center was thereupon opened in Weston, Connecticut, greatly facilitating a closer relationship with the schools of New York City's exurbia. In an attempt to expand their teacher-training activities, project members then opened a third center, this one at Webster College, St. Louis, Missouri. Since 1961 the project has been supported by funds from the National Science Foundation and the U.S. Office of Education.

The over-all objective of the Madison project, according to its director, Robert B. Davis, has been "to use mathematics as an approach to the task of improving the quality of pre-college education, particularly in relation to giving students a deeper sense of involvement in the process of their own education, and to increasing the sense of vitality and relevance of educational experiences."[6]

6. Robert B. Davis, *The Madison Project* (rev. ed.). St. Louis: Webster College, 1965.

Specifically, the project has sought to broaden the curriculum, especially for grades 2-8, by introducing some of the fundamental concepts of algebra and coordinate geometry, ideas of logic, and some work on the relations of mathematics to physical science. It has also sought to infuse a more creative flavor into the curriculum. To achieve these objectives, project members have constructed a cohesive program of supplementary work in mathematics that is not intended to replace the existing curriculum but rather to enrich and improve it, and to be used in conjunction with it. Experience has shown that the materials are most effective if they are phased in gradually, at the rate of one hour a week until the program is well established.

Reflecting the staff's belief in the importance of creative involvement and learning by discovery, Madison project materials are designed to provide the student with mathematical experiences that help him to discover patterns in abstract situations; to learn such basic mathematical ideas as variables, functions, graphs, implications, and others; and to acquire a reasonable mastery of the most important techniques. The student, furthermore, is led to realize that mathematics is incomplete and open-ended, that abstract rational analysis and an "educated" intuition are valuable tools, and that mathematics can be fun and a worthwhile subject to pursue.

Teacher preparation is a central activity of the Madison project. Class materials form an essential component of pre-service and in-service training, and of undergraduate and graduate teacher-education programs at Webster College. Workshops and summer institutes at project centers and other cities are used to acquaint teachers with the new lessons and the Madison approach.

In order to achieve nationwide dissemination of its products, the project has recorded on tape and motion-picture film actual classroom lessons with children that teachers can view and use in preparing their own lessons. A packaged course for in-service education, consisting of films and printed matter, has been prepared for teaching personnel who cannot avail themselves of the assistance of project members or professional mathematicians. In Chicago alone the project's teacher-education efforts involve some 18,000 public school teachers.

Publications include two textbooks, *Discovery in Mathematics* and

Explorations in Mathematics, and a number of pamphlets, reports, and upwards of fifteen films.

Evaluation procedures to assess the progress of students have included standardized tests, classroom observations, teacher-made tests, and interviews with children. An extensive evaluation of project materials is scheduled for the near future, as is the development of materials for individualized study in grades 6-12. Evaluation problems are compounded, as in many other projects, by the difficulty of separating "pure" Madison math from the particular content and method the project seeks to augment or replace.

University of Illinois Committee on School Mathematics

The Committee on School Mathematics developed as a result of the interest of three colleges (Education, Engineering, and Liberal Arts and Sciences) at the University of Illinois in improving their freshman courses. This interest subsequently shifted to high-school mathematics. From 1951 through 1961, the work of the committee was supported by funds from the University of Illinois, the U.S. Office of Education, the National Science Foundation (for summer institutes), and the Carnegie Corporation. During these ten years, materials for grades 9-12 were produced and tested. The second phase of this program, the preparation of materials for grades 7 and 8 and for a new high-school geometry program, began in 1962 and is being supported by the National Science Foundation.

The committee set out to present mathematics as a consistent, unified discipline; to lead students to discover principles for themselves; and to assure the development of the manipulative skills necessary for problem solving. The UICSM program emphasizes "learning by discovery," with the student working out the mathematics rather than being told about it. The student need not verbalize his discovery; in fact, verbalization, for communication and proof, is to come only after the student has become thoroughly familiar with the generalization and has had adequate opportunity to test and refine it.

The four-year sequential program has been developed through eleven units as follows: 1) the arithmetic of real numbers; 2) pronumerals, generalizations, and algebraic manipulations; 3) equations and inequations, applications; 4) ordered pairs and graphs; 5) relations and functions; 6) geometry; 7) mathematical induction; 8) sequences; 9) exponential and logarithmic functions; 10) circular functions and trigonometry; and 11) polynomial functions and complex numbers. Units 1-4 are intended for the first year (grade 9), units 5-6 for the second, units 7-8 for the third, and units 9-11 for the fourth (grade 12). There is a teachers' edition for each unit, consisting of the students' edition plus commentary pages, providing mathematical background material and teaching suggestions, together with answers to the problems in the text. Both editions have been published by D. C. Heath and Co. Also available from the same publisher are new versions of the first three years of the curriculum.

The UICSM program is designed for all students, but it is assumed that many will drop mathematics after a year or two, leaving for the last two years only those students who are somewhat more interested in mathematics. Some schools report satisfactory use of the 9th-grade materials with gifted 8th-grade pupils or even with very gifted 7th-grade students.

Materials planned for the second phase of the project include a two-year sequence in vector geometry which develops most of the standard theorems (and some unusual ones) of the geometry of the plane and of three-dimensional space and of trigonometry through a study of the properties of the vector space of translations. In these materials the process of choosing postulates is a very slow and deliberate one, so that the courses also serve to illustrate both the arbitrary nature and the power of an elegant abstract mathematical system.

The UICSM project during the last three years has developed mathematics materials for 7th and 8th-grade students who are under-achievers. These students often have little motivation and no more than a 4th or 5th-grade level of reading ability. Project members hope that students finishing this two-year program will be able to perform at the level expected of beginning 9th-grade algebra students. The bulk of the 7th-grade material deals with the arithmetic of rational numbers in their fractional, decimal, and percentage forms—i.e., with the basic components of the upper elementary mathematics curriculum. The 8th-grade program consists of lessons in informal geometry and algebra, an introduction to real numbers, and continues the development of skills and ideas begun in the 7th-grade program.

These courses have been taught on an experimental basis in eighty-five classes by teachers who have attended a three-week orientation seminar. Attendance at these training sessions by trial-class teachers is a regular feature of the project's teacher-training activities. Teachers report once weekly during the tryout period and are visited by a project member once a month. Materials are currently being revised and are not generally available.

The effectiveness of the UICSM program has not been fully tested. This is due partly to the difficulty entailed in evaluating such goals, for example, as "an intuitive grasp of fundamental principles," partly to the absence of criteria for comparing programs. Students in the UICSM courses, however, do at least as well as students in traditional mathematics on tests designed for the latter.

What the UICSM has produced so far is a promising beginning. The director, Max Beberman, is very interested in programmed materials and computer technology, and the computer analysis of the systems approach to the teaching-learning situation that his group has started should prove valuable in further curriculum revision.

University of Illinois Arithmetic Project
at Educational Services Incorporated

The development and viewpoint of the University of Illinois Arithmetic Project have been closely identified with its director, David A. Page. The project's central purpose is to help teachers teach children the kind of mathematics that youngsters find exciting; or, put another way, to help teachers stimulate children over the prospect of adventures in mathematics, which, above all, should not be confused with a body of manipulative skills.

"The true mathematician, as contrasted with the expert in computation, is uninspired by the prospect of performing routine, repetitive tasks, just as a true artist would not wish to paint many copies of the

31

same picture . . . the mathematician's primary creative activity is the study of patterns, relationships, forms, and structures in systems of numbers, geometrical figures, functions, and other objects of interest."[7]

The project has been variously supported by the University of Illinois, the Carnegie Corporation, and the National Science Foundation; it is now operating in association with ESI. It is engaged in creating on film and on paper a series of four courses in mathematics for elementary-school teachers, and in adapting these for use by universities and other institutions concerned with teacher training. Materials already produced and available include such publications as *Ways to Find How Many; Do Something About Estimation; Number Lines, Functions, and Fundamental Topics;* and *Maneuvers on Lattices: An Example of Intermediate Invention.* The subtitle of the latter illustrates one of the project's principal ideas.

According to David Page, more topics or "intermediate inventions" are needed before adequate mathematics programs for schools can be formulated, or even before worthwhile discussions can be held on such topics as discovery methods, the cognitive process, grade placement, articulation, and the objectives of mathematics curricula in the schools. A good intermediate invention, for instance, such as a table or lattice of numbers, provides a focal point for teacher and class and a beginning point for mathematical exploration. Children are encouraged to guess, invent, and employ mathematical principles without restrictions of having to solve one specific problem or to find one correct answer (already known to the teacher). Thus children develop an intuition for genuine mathematical ideas and a sense of power with respect to certain mathematical properties and operations. Mathematical principles are not labeled. A child may discover and use the commutative law but he is not immediately called upon to verbalize it. He may invent words for it or, until such time as the technical term facilitates communication with others, simply sense it. Topics, or intermediate inventions, are designed to appeal to the whole range of elementary-school (and even secondary-school) students and are not arranged or identified by grades.

---

7. Franz E. Hohn, "Teaching Creativity in Mathematics," *Arithmetic Teacher,* March, 1961, p. 102.

Course materials do not consist of "new" mathematics but rather of novel ways of doing old mathematics—of new structures and schemes that contain significant mathematical ideas as well as problems that children can solve. As project members realized that topics suitable for elementary grades can also be used to provide challenging work for students in high school and above, and that there is little difference between what interests the average, the handicapped, and the gifted child, they have begun to extend their work to disadvantaged and to blind children and to high-school students.

In cooperation with ESI's Pre-College Program for Students from Low-Income Families, which was instituted to halt the high dropout rate of undergraduates at predominantly Negro colleges, special materials have been developed for students about to enter college. Working with the Perkins School for the Blind in Boston, project members have assisted in preparing experimental Braille and other tactile materials and in adapting certain course sections for use with blind children.

Page and his colleagues are convinced that significantly different classroom material cannot be taught successfully until teachers have been thoroughly prepared. For the last two years, therefore, the project has conducted a series of sixteen-week institutes for groups of about 100 teachers from nearby cities. Weekly sessions center on demonstration classes taught by project members or on films of such classes, and on extensive written lessons. This is followed by discussions of what has been seen and learned. Teachers are encouraged to try out ideas they have learned at the institute in their own classrooms as soon as possible. Institute participants are given an opportunity to teach under project supervision.

These institutes serve several functions: they provide a prototype of the course that the project is producing; they afford project teachers valuable practice in demonstration teaching before they teach in front of the camera; and they provide an invaluable, though informal, means of evaluating the project's work and its impact upon schools. All together some 500 teachers have been trained at the institutes.

The project's emphasis on teaching and on the children's sensing the elegance of mathematics is enhanced by the substantial use of motion pictures in the course. Much of its work has to be grasped intuitively.

The observer of a well-taught class feels inspired to do likewise—though to do exactly likewise would be to miss the point of the exercise. Teachers, characteristically, develop their own style as they use the Arithmetic Project's materials.

University of Maryland Mathematics Project

The University of Maryland Mathematics Project was established in 1957 with the support of the Carnegie Corporation. Its objective was to prepare experimental mathematics courses for grades 7 and 8 so that junior high-school students could benefit from the previously developed new mathematics courses for the senior high-school level. To this initial mandate, the project has over the years added a concern for elementary-school teachers as well as a continuing interest in the learning problems of mathematics.

The first three years, 1957-60, were taken up with the development, testing, and revision of 7th and 8th-grade courses. The new materials, published in 1961 under the title *Mathematics for the Junior High School*, Books I and II, place great emphasis on number systems and attempt to help students recognize the properties of a mathematical structure. The usual topics taught in these grades are approached from a fresh point of view, and the student is introduced to the elements of mathematical logic. Evaluation studies have shown that students in the Maryland Project courses did as well on traditional tests as students in the traditional courses, and better on the tests specifically designed to measure achievement in the UMMaP courses.

In 1962, supported by a grant from the National Science Foundation, UMMaP began to work on experimental courses in mathematics for elementary-school teachers. The same procedure was used as before: materials were prepared in draft form and submitted to trial teaching and revisions, and *Mathematics for Elementary School Teachers*, Books I and II, was published in 1965. One volume deals with algebra, the other with geometry, but instead of presenting the prospective teacher with a series of mathematical "truths" to be committed to memory, they assist him in using the discovery method and in finding clues to support a conclusion that he himself might have arrived at.

Work on the project's third concern—learning research—began in 1960. Activities during the first two years were under the direction of Robert Gagné, now with the University of California, Berkeley. Stanford Erickson of the University of Michigan's psychology department served as a consultant during the third year; and Bruce Tuckman of Rutgers University is the consultant for present research efforts. Funds for these endeavors are derived from the sale of the 7th and 8th-grade texts.

One aspect of UMMaP involves the careful programing of each learning step so that a hierarchical structure of "learning sets" (subordinate knowledges) is produced. A good program mediates learning so that it ensures a positive transfer from lower-level to higher-level learning sets for each individual learner. A study by Gagné[8] confirmed this learning-set theory in an investigation of 136 students in four 7th-grade classes, using *Mathematics for the Junior High School*. Furthermore, it showed that students of widely varying ability were able to move forward successfully in a carefully programed sequence.

A follow-up study that used a unit on non-metric geometry introduced two variables: exercises of varying levels of difficulty, and the time needed for the completion of the program. Five different programs were administered to each of four participating classes. After an interval of two weeks, students took an achievement test and a test to study the validity of the learning-set structure. Retention was tested eight weeks later. The aim was to examine what effect the various programs had on final achievement of the task and on retention, and to verify the learning-set structure. The findings[9] once again confirmed the learning-set theory, but by uncovering a significant difference in achievement in the retention test raised questions about the nature and role of repetition.

The third study therefore was designed to examine the role that repetition plays in learning. The focus was changed from programed instruction to the classroom and the individual student, but results so far have been inconclusive.

8. Robert M. Gagné and associates, "Factors in Acquiring Knowledge of a Mathematical Task," *Psychological Monographs: General and Applied,* Vol. 76, No. 7, 1962.

9. Robert M. Gagné and Otto C. Bassler, "Study of Retention of Some Topics of Elementary Nongeometric Geometry," *Journal of Educational Psychology,* Vol. 54, 1962, pp. 123-131.

Project director John Mayor attributes the success of Maryland's course development program to the fact that cooperating psychologists, mathematicians, and teachers all approached their assignments as a team. This same team approach will be used in future learning-research studies in the hope that it will help solve some of the problems that still plague learning and curriculum design.

Experimental Teaching of Mathematics in the Elementary School

Computer-Based Mathematics Instruction

Patrick Suppes of Stanford University has for many years been interested in the introduction of non-traditional mathematical concepts into the elementary-school curriculum. In 1959, as director of a project for the Experimental Teaching of Mathematics in the Elementary School, he turned his attention to the basic arithmetic curriculum and the development of a mathematics program for children in kindergarten and the first eight grades.

The central concept of this new curriculum is that of a set. Suppes views sets as appropriate for young children because sets are more concrete than numbers and, in addition, facilitate mathematically precise definitions. Although major emphasis in the course is on the concepts, laws, and skills of arithmetic, content from both algebra and particularly geometry has been included. The lessons stress exact language and are based on the premise that children in the primary grades can learn much more mathematics than is traditionally assumed. Workbooks and teachers' manuals for grades K-6 have been published in a series of books called *Sets and Numbers;* work is continuing on materials for grades 7 and 8, which, upon completion, will become part of the series.

A closely related project on the teaching of mathematical logic began about the same time. Its purpose was to introduce academically gifted 5th and 6th graders to "modern mathematics and mathematical methods at a level that is rigorous but simple enough in presentation and context to permit a fairly easy comprehension." Course materials were divided into two parts, the first dealing with the sentential theory of inference and the second with the logic of quantifications. Carefully designed experiments showed that elementary-school students, taught by teachers trained in logic, can score nearly as high on logic tests as Stanford University students. A revised edition of the experimental text, entitled *First Course in Mathematics,* is commercially available.

Funds for these efforts (and other relevant studies not discussed here) came from the National Science Foundation, the Office of Education, and the Carnegie Corporation.

Since 1963, Suppes and his associates have attempted to construct a computer-based curriculum in elementary-school mathematics. This endeavor became the sole concern of the Computer-Based Mathematics Instruction (CBMI) project, also supported by the National Science Foundation and directed by Suppes.

Several years of research in learning theory convinced Suppes that one of the most important (and also most neglected) principles of learning is the existence of differences in individual rates of learning. "Single-minded concentration on individual differences," he feels, "could result in the greatest improvement in subject-matter learning." Computer technology seems one way in which such improvement can be brought about. Since each student works independently of the progress of the other students, he can proceed at his own pace. Computer-based teaching machines can also provide immediate reinforcement and correction, giving a reasonably close imitation of a teaching situation in which a tutor works with one individual student. In addition, a computer facility permits a deeper analysis of transfer phenomena as the child moves from one mathematical concept to another.

During the last three years, members of the Computer-Based Mathematics Instruction project have developed experimental programs (in mathematical logic) for grades 1, 4, and 6. The 1st and 4th-grade materials follow the content and sequence of the *Sets and Numbers* books, except that the 4th-grade course is constructed for use by children who have had no previous introduction to the new mathematics.

The first-grade program consists of approximately fifty sections, each introducing a new "concept." Problems to be solved follow each section and the number of problems varies from concept to concept. As the child proceeds through the material, review problems test his knowledge of the previous concepts. If he responds correctly to half of the problems, he will continue through the review to the next concept; if he fails more than half the questions, the computer will register these data and on the next day present him with an intensive review of the particular concepts. In this way the child is continually tested on his retention of previously learned subject matter.

The instructional units of the 4th-grade material consist of a number of learning blocks, each of which contains a major concept and several problems to be worked by the student. Of two units that have been completed, the first includes such topics as addition, subtraction, multiplication, division, and word problems and equations. The second unit deals with operations on numbers and with the commutative, associative, and distributive laws. The student has to meet specified criteria before he can proceed to more advanced problems; failure to meet these criteria results in return to remedial material.

The 6th-grade lessons, based on the previously developed sequence in mathematical logic, make full use of the versatility of computer-based teaching machines. Since such a facility allows immediate evaluation of response data and accepts any valid step in a proof, it is possible to present new stimulus items that are contingent upon the student's immediately preceding performance.

The student in this course is first presented with logical symbols, which are interpreted for him. He is then asked to view the symbols as concrete objects and, using arbitrary rules of derivation introduced one at a time, to manipulate the symbols as he would pieces on a game board. At the next stage he learns to regard the "pieces" as carriers of the possible truth values of "true" or "false"; through a number of steps he is shown that the rules initially introduced as arbitrary never allow the derivation of a false conclusion from true premises. Subsequent lessons inform him about the methods of conditional proof, indirect proof, and biconditional replacement. Finally, they acquaint the student with the formal concepts of arguments and consistency or inconsistency of sets of premises. A discussion on the development of a logical system concludes the course.

Evaluation plans for CBMI texts include the use of modern learning-theory's standard statistical tools, including general and standard achievement tests. Long-term details, however, have not yet been worked out.

Teacher preparation has played an important part in the project for Experimental Teaching of Mathematics in the Elementary School; CBMI at present has no provisions for such activities, though plans for the future indicate an interest in teacher training.

Materials for computer-assisted instruction have been used in Stanford's computer-based laboratory for learning and teaching. They have recently been introduced in a neighboring elementary school, where a new system of sixteen terminals has been installed, permitting sixteen students to work independently at the same time.

There is little doubt that the essential idea of computer-based learning —individual accommodation—offers one of the most revolutionary possibilities for curriculum reform.

Physical and Biological Sciences

Serious rethinking of the natural science curriculum dates back to the mid-1950's when dissatisfaction with what was being taught in the schools ran high. Professor Jerrold Zacharias of the Massachusetts Institute of Technology brought scientists together for discussions from which emerged the common pattern of cooperation between scholars and teachers. They turned their attention upon the "big three" sciences of the high-school curriculum: biology, chemistry, and physics. Most of the work and supporting funds have been poured into the four courses described below.

Experience with the new curricula uncovered some needs that subsequent projects (not described in detail here) have attempted to meet. The Introductory Physical Science course, for example, being developed by ESI (the sponsors of the PSSC course in physics) primarily for the 9th grade, was conceived in response to teachers who felt that such new programs as those of the BSCS, CBA, CHEM Study, and PSSC could be more effectively taught if they were preceded by a course designed to acquaint students with an attitude of inquiry as well as with some of the most basic experimental and mathematical skills. Harvard Project Physics, initiated in 1964, is developing a senior high-school physics course that relates the subject matter to other fields, reveals the humanistic aspects of science, and examines some of the effects science has had on society. There is some expectation that this course might check the decline in physics enrollment at both high-school and college levels. Project Physics personnel hope to have available by 1968 a thoroughly tested and integrated high-school physics curriculum and an evaluative report on its effectiveness. The Secondary School Science Project, set up in 1962 at Princeton University, focuses on the nature of the physical world and encourages the students to employ the principles of chemistry, physics, geology, astronomy, and mathematics in their problem-solving activities. The course, "Time, Space, and Matter," is designed for the 10th grade.

The innovative thrust in science content and method of approach now seems to be at the elementary-school level where the curriculum based on secondary-school assumptions appears not to be working very well. The three major projects, described below, have moved away from the single discipline approach, each in its own distinctive way. They have been chosen for a more detailed description here because they aptly illustrate some of the recurring problems and issues that will be discussed in Section III.

Two other projects are worth mentioning. The University of Illinois Elementary-School Science Project[10] offers an interesting approach both to organizing content around fundamental elements of the discipline (primarily astronomy) and to introducing the student to the thought processes of scientists. The Minnesota Mathematics and Science Teaching Project (MINNEMAST) is designed to produce a coordinated mathematics and science program for grades K-9. In the words of its director, Paul Rosenbloom, "It is the only major project that coordinates science and mathematics and at the same time is developing college subject matter and methods courses for the pre-service and in-service education of teachers."

---

10. See *School Curriculum Reform, op. cit.,* pp. 35-37.

Because no single science runs the length of the K-12 curriculum the way mathematics does, the physical and biological sciences present some troublesome and fascinating problems and issues: How many years should high-school students study science? Which of the sciences and how many of them should be included in the elementary-school curriculum? What common features in the sciences might be learned best in an integrated course? The projects that follow are attempting to answer some of these questions.

Biological Sciences Curriculum Study

The work of the Biological Sciences Curriculum Study is unique in that there are three sets of parallel materials—a Green, Yellow, and Blue version—each differing in approach but each organized around the same unifying concepts, and intended for the average and above-average student. A fourth version, for the lower-ability student, has just been published. The study was organized in 1959 by the Education Committee of the American Institute of Biological Sciences, with Bentley Glass as chairman of a twenty-seven-member steering committee, and Arnold Grobman as director. In the fall of 1965, Grobman assumed the chairmanship and William V. Mayer became the study's director. Headquarters are at the University of Colorado. The steering committee and working groups are composed of biologists, a substantial representation of high-school teachers, and various educational specialists. Activities have been supported by $8 million of National Science Foundation funds, with the international aspects of the program receiving smaller amounts also from the Rockefeller and Asia foundations.

Early in its work, the committee set forth some basic agreements, such as the view that biology taught in the schools in 1960 was from twenty to a hundred years behind the available knowledge in science. It also recognized that to meet the demands of a modern curriculum in biology, some sensitive topics, such as evolution and human reproduction, would need to be included. The committee further agreed that biology must be updated and presented as a changing science, that cut-and-dried laboratory experiments should be abandoned and instead students should be involved in discovery. Since the diversity of the life sciences suggested, in turn, diversity of treatment in the schools, committee members decided that certain central biological themes and methods of inquiry should permeate the treatment of content. The committee also suggested that the content of the three basic versions should be within the grasp of a majority of students at the 10th-grade level.

Nine unifying themes run through each of the three versions of BSCS biology: change in living things (evolution); the diversity of type and unity of pattern in living things; the genetic continuity of life; the biological roots of behavior; the complementarity of organism and environment; the complementarity of structure and function; regulation and homeostasis, the maintenance of life in the face of change; science as inquiry; and the intellectual history of biological concepts. Approximately two-thirds of the content is the same in the three programs for the average and above-average students. While there is a difference in approach and emphasis, each of the versions represents a one-year general biology course.

The Green version emphasizes the biological community, beginning with the complexity and diversity of life and coming to cellular structure relatively late in the course. Major topics are the following: the biosphere dissected, evolution, behavior, and man. The Yellow version, emphasizing cellular biology at the outset, divides the subject matter into seven sections: cells, micro-organisms, plants, animals, genetics, evolution, and ecology. The Blue version stresses physiological and biochemical evolutionary processes, with emphasis on the contributions that molecular biology has made to the general understanding of the universe. The topics are: biology—the interaction of facts and ideas; evolution of the cell; the evolving organism; multicellular organisms—energy utilization; multicellular organisms—integrative systems; and higher levels of organization. The materials for the lower-ability student treat the same themes as the other versions, but the presentation is made at a slower pace and a greater variety of teaching techniques is suggested. All versions are available through commercial publishers.

BSCS courses differ from traditional courses in that they place greater emphasis on molecular and cellular biology, on the community and world biome, and on the study of populations. They stress investigation and principles, and the universal rather than the applied aspects of biology. In addition, students spend a far greater proportion of their time in the laboratory in exploratory and investigative experiments.

Materials published include textbooks for each of the three versions, laboratory manuals, teachers' handbooks and guides, a series of laboratory "block" units (each consisting of integrated experiments on special topics of biology), investigation booklets containing problems for which there are no published solutions, a pamphlet series on specific biological topics, a bulletin series on biological education, films on laboratory techniques, and information media including a film, and a Newsletter and International News Notes series. To be released in the near future are single-topic films. The laboratory block is not so much for enrichment as it is an alternative device, taking the student out of six weeks of regular classwork into investigation of a single area of biology, thus guiding him to his own discoveries and conclusions. A second-level course, designed to follow the regular BSCS course, is available through the normal commercial channels.

The Biological Sciences Curriculum Study has made substantial progress in developing and using tests that determine the attainment of course objectives. The results of successive years of evaluation have satisfied the committee that average and above-average students performed adequately on achievement tests based on BSCS materials. Test data substantiate reports from teachers that the regular version programs, intended for 10th graders, probably are not suitable for average 9th-grade students but could be handled by above-average 9th graders in optimal school settings. Extensive evaluation of materials is continuing and is reported periodically in the Newsletter.

During the developmental phase the teachers using the materials had been required to obtain special preparation through in-service institutes, summer workshops, special college courses, or BSCS briefing sessions. But the fundamental readiness of teachers to teach the new biology depends largely on the establishment of collegiate programs, including new content and the necessary pedagogy, and their introduction into pre-service teacher education. The Committee on Undergraduate Education in the Biological Sciences (CUEBS) at George Washington University is concerned with the improvement of the collegiate curriculum in biology and maintains a liaison with the BSCS.

Chemical Bond Approach Project

In the summer of 1957 a small group of chemists met at Reed College in Portland, Oregon, to pursue and act upon their mutual interest in improving high-school and college freshman chemistry. Four years of writing during the summer months and of testing the materials during the school year resulted in the publication of a new chemistry textbook and a laboratory guide for use in high schools. This endeavor has been supported by the National Science Foundation.

Laurence E. Strong, who has been directing the CBA project at Earlham College (Richmond, Indiana), sums up the thinking behind the present course as follows:

"The Chemical Bond Approach Project is an attempt to develop an introductory chemistry course which presents modern chemistry to beginning students. The presentation is intended to give students a preliminary understanding of what chemistry is about, rather than simply an encyclopedic collection of chemical reactions and laboratory techniques, or a mere overview of diverse conclusions held by chemists today. Such a course must be an organized one in which the pattern reflects the structure of the discipline itself. Since conceptual schemes play a major role in the organization of chemistry today, the organization of the course in chemistry is best based on conceptual schemes."[11]

The central theme of the CBA course is chemical bonds, the ties between atoms. As one writer puts it, "The making and breaking of these ties between atoms is chemistry."[12] With such central concepts, the student can be expected to relate previous and new learning effectively and to use it in dealing with new problems. The project set out to prepare text and laboratory materials that would introduce students to the chemistry of today.

An attempt is made throughout the course to present the student with the logical implications of experimental fact. This is done mostly

11. Laurence E. Strong, "Facts, Students, Ideas," *Journal of Chemical Education,* 39 (March, 1962), p. 126.

12. Robert E. Henze, "New Developments in High School Chemistry," *The New School Science,* p. 41. Washington, D. C.: American Association for the Advancement of Science, 1963.

through the discussion of mental models, which are introduced as logical devices, based on a set of assumptions that are consistent with themselves and with the facts.

The course emphasizes laboratory work, which is designed to develop in the student the ability to identify a problem, to design an experiment that will shed light on this problem, to carry out the technical operations of the experiment, and to arrive at a conclusion based on analysis of his own data. Assistance is gradually withdrawn until the student finally performs all of the steps independently, employing techniques he has learned from exploration of earlier problems.

The text and the laboratory program run parallel and reinforce each other. The CBA course puts rather heavy demands on teachers who are working with it for the first time. The content itself should present no unusual problems as it is intended for the average high-school students of chemistry, but to get behind the material to understand the point of view is most important. Whether the course actually is suitable for all students is a point of debate. Nevertheless, students with relatively low aptitude scores have done surprisingly well on special achievement examinations devised by CBA writers in cooperation with the Educational Testing Service. Students in conventional programs do poorly on the special tests when compared with CBA students. However, the CBA students do slightly less well than students in conventional programs when the two groups are compared on conventional tests, such as the College Entrance Examination Board's chemistry exam.

There are, in addition to the text and the laboratory guide, a teachers' guide and some programed materials. At the outset, scrambling techniques of programing were used but current materials are primarily linear. It is interesting and significant that the CBA project, like other curriculum ventures beset with the many problems inherent in reform, is looking to programed instruction—another new movement in education—for what it can contribute to curriculum improvement.

Like so many other curriculum projects, the CBA has not yet been integrated into the pre-service education of teachers, or into the preparation of educators who will advance the cause of science education. Reforms of this kind call for the restructuring of higher education, an undertaking that extends far beyond the scope of a single discipline.

Chemical Education Material Study

The Chemical Education Material Study stemmed from an *ad hoc* committee appointed by the American Chemical Society to study the need for revising the chemistry course at the high-school level. Until the summer of 1963, J. Arthur Campbell of Harvey Mudd College served as project director. Headquarters were then transferred to the University of California, Berkeley, where the work is being carried on by George C. Pimentel, who also served as editor of the textbook.

Considering that the first meeting of the CHEM Study steering committee was not held until January, 1960, the production of several experimental paperbound editions, leading to the publication of a hardcover book, available for the school year 1963-64, was an amazing accomplishment. During 1965-66 approximately 350,000 students in the United States were using CHEM Study materials.

The project set out to reduce the gap between scientists and teachers in the understanding of science; to stimulate able high-school students to continue the study of science in college; to encourage teachers to keep up with their fields through courses on the new knowledge in science; and to develop an understanding of the importance of science by students who will discontinue their chemistry after high school. These purposes are being accomplished through the preparation of effective teaching materials: textbooks, a manual of laboratory experiments, a teachers' guide, films, and supplementary reading materials.

The course begins with an overview of chemistry, emphasizing the atomic-molecular nature of substances. Explanations of the behavior of substances are developed according to the theory of atoms and of energy changes. Students are introduced to the periodic table, its uses and how it was actually devised. The course then moves into the topics of energy, reaction rate, equilibrium, acids and bases, and oxidation-reduction. Later, the student studies bonding and structural relationships in the various states of matter, together with their influence on chemical reactivity. The course concludes with a substantial introduction to organic and descriptive chemistry, with frequent application of the principles covered earlier. Throughout, the concepts are introduced in the laboratory and then are developed and tied together through kinetic theory and atomic-molecular concepts of behavior and matter.

The CBA textbook presents students with an exercise in speculation and theorizing. The CHEM Study presents students with an initial exercise in observation. They are asked to observe a burning candle and to note all of their observations. Whereas most students record a dozen or so items, a professional chemist's report (in the appendix of the textbook) lists fifty-three observations.

As with the CBA project, the CHEM Study relies heavily on experimentation in the laboratory. In contrast to the CBA, however, CHEM Study builds the laboratory right into the sequence of the text; principles are developed through students' laboratory discoveries. Chemical reactions that cannot be done in a classroom laboratory are presented in a series of films. Like the laboratory activity, these films are designed to be used not casually but at specific times during the course. Subject matter of the films is developed by specialists (who often appear in the films) and the films are then produced commercially. Several of these productions have won coveted awards.

Though the present text has been released in collaboration with a commercial publishing house, the materials are still under the control of the project. Publishers, however, may borrow from its content upon request and are encouraged by the staff's liberal policy to do so. Since the project's main purpose has always been to bring chemistry up to date in every possible way, there has been no thought of its becoming a continuing producer of materials. Present plans are directed toward generating a variety of revisions based upon CHEM Study materials but under the normal author-publisher relationship.

In retrospect it is clear that the excellence of the curriculum study materials, both of CBA and of CHEM Study, stems from the high caliber of the writers. As George Pimentel sees it, "to avoid the need for another such 'crash' program, high-school textbook publishers must accept responsibility for attracting truly outstanding authors, including university-level, practicing scientists as well as experienced teachers. The prevailing, strong influence of the in-house 'science-editor' must be relaxed together with the traditional reluctance to innovate and to remove obsolete material. We must not return to another generation of textbooks subservient to national testing programs and last year's market place."

Physical Science Study Committee

The Physical Science Study Committee, in developing a first physics course for high-school students, has acted as a pioneer in many areas of the curriculum reform movement: in the effective involvement of scholars and teachers, in the search for truly fundamental concepts, in the development of films, and in the packaging of an instructional program. PSSC's activities, initially centered at the Massachusetts Institute of Technology, led to the formation of Educational Services Inc. at Newton, Massachusetts.

A central component of the course is the laboratory in which students gain firsthand experience in discovering and verifying physical phenomena. The program presents facts that are different from those traditionally included in an elementary physics course, but seeks concepts that are understood and used, not just asserted. The committee has worked out a comprehensive set of means for achieving the purposes of its course: a textbook, laboratory experiments and simplified apparatus, films, achievement tests, books on special topics, and a teachers' guide for classroom and laboratory activities. A second edition of these course materials is now available, reflecting the experience of five years of classroom teaching but leaving the substance of the course substantially the same.

The course consists of four parts, each one building on the preceding part. Part I deals with the fundamental concepts of time, space, and matter; Part II with a detailed examination of light; Part III with motion; and Part IV with electricity and the physics of the atom. Students count, measure, observe; they learn about, construct, and test conceptual models; and finally they arrive at a reasonably sophisticated model of atoms. They come to see that physics is not fixed or static but that it evolves from the inquiries and basic research of scientists.

Where textbooks, class discussion, and laboratory work leave off, films take over. The films are not of the usual "enrichment" sort. Some introduce the student to an area that he will traverse later; others present the more difficult portions of the course. Painstaking care has gone into the production of each film, be it the portrayal of physical phenomena or of investigators at work.

Teacher institutes during the summer and school year are an integral part of the PSSC physics program. Since the first year of operation, 1957-58, when eight teachers and 300 students used the course, it has mushroomed. Approximately 5,000 teachers and 200,000 students, or 50 per cent of all secondary students enrolled in physics classes in the U.S., participated during 1965-66. Many more teachers are using parts of the course in conjunction with conventional physics textbooks, and interest has spread even to foreign countries. Translations of the PSSC textbook, either in full or in part, and of the laboratory guide into Danish, French, Hebrew, Italian, Japanese, Korean, Norwegian, Portuguese, Spanish, Swedish, and Serbo-Croatian have been published; a translation of the teachers' guide into Spanish is in process.

Evaluation of the program confronts the obvious query: can its effectiveness be appraised by using conventional tests? The committee's answer is an emphatic "No." Mimeographed articles contrast the objectives of the PSSC course with the objectives of conventional physics courses, revealing the limitations of conventional tests in attempting evaluative comparisons. An examination prepared and administered by the College Entrance Examination Board has been used to compare students in PSSC with those in conventional physics classes.

Students who take this new physics course, like students in the other new high-school curricula, move on to college courses based mostly on the old materials. There is no evidence to suggest that the new curriculum high-school graduates are in any way at a disadvantage, although they sometimes have indicated a dissatisfaction with their college fare. The Physical Science Study Committee points to the need for revising the college physics curriculum if PSSC students are to be adequately challenged, and if college courses are to keep pace with current thought in physics education. There are increasing signs that this collegiate reform has started.

Science Curriculum Improvement Study

The Science Curriculum Improvement Study has been funded since 1959 by a grant from the National Science Foundation. The director is Robert Karplus of the University of California, Berkeley. The program is based on fundamental science concepts and a methodology which emphasizes pupil experimentation and observation.

The purpose of the study is to develop a teaching program for the primary grades that will increase the scientific literacy of the school population, i.e., that will provide the individual with sufficient knowledge and experience to enable him to understand the scientific attitudes, procedures, and concepts that will play an increasingly significant part in his daily life.

Karplus and his colleagues believe that many concrete experiences are needed in the early years to enable the child to build a conceptual framework for dealing with later ideas and knowledge. Special care, therefore, is taken to acquaint children with specific examples of objects and organisms, to let them examine natural phenomena, and to help them develop skills in manipulating equipment and recording data. Instead of being supplied with correct answers, children are encouraged to think for themselves, to respond creatively to problems presented to them, and to arrive at conclusions on the basis of their own observation and interpretation of evidence.

The course outline is related to the hierarchial level of abstraction in the program. Stressing the concept-oriented nature of his study, Karplus warns that abstractions on earlier levels have to be grasped before those on succeeding levels can become meaningful. First-level abstractions contain the conceptions of matter (including activity and growth in living matter) and variation in one property among similar objects. Second-level abstractions deal with the concepts of interaction, relativity, and ecosystem. Energy, equilibrium, behavior, reproduction, and evolution of living organisms are among the concepts of third-level abstractions.

Eight instructional units for grades K-6 have been produced and are currently being tried out in four schools in the San Francisco Bay area. Materials for the first four grades are available from the project and are in their fourth year of trial teaching. Grade placement is less important than sequence in determining when a unit is taught. Lessons are organized in a sequential fashion and assume an increasing understanding of the concept being developed. Students' manuals are designed for specific instructional purposes.

SCIS personnel are keenly aware of how important teacher preparation is for the teaching of science. To meet this essential requirement they have organized several orientation conferences, conducted an in-service course, and prepared a teacher-training package containing students' and teachers' manuals for specific topics, audio-visual aids, and kits of equipment for certain experiments. These materials are not yet available to the public.

Current plans include the development of a sequential life science program for the primary grades and of materials for the physical life sciences for the upper grades. Additional testing with a larger group of teachers and pupils is planned to take place at four new trial centers at Columbia's Teachers College, the University of California at Los Angeles, the University of Oklahoma, and the University of Hawaii; a commercial edition of SCIS units, published by D. C. Heath and Co., will be used. Feedback received from teachers at these centers will be considered in further revisions of SCIS materials.

Precise evaluation of the project's effect has been difficult since the program does not state objectives in great detail. The learning opportunities described in the manuals, which provide for pupils' activity and involvement, have been found to make the children respond to problems with answers based on evidence rather than on guesswork. While the program was designed to utilize the principles of child development, its impact will be evident only after students have participated in it for several years.

Elementary Science Study

Concerned with raising the quality and broadening the scope of elementary education, Educational Services Incorporated in 1960 launched the Elementary Science Study. Financial support from the National Science Foundation and the Sloan Foundation has enabled the project members to develop a number of experimental units designed to fulfill a threefold purpose: to contribute to a more balanced curriculum by bringing science into the classroom of the early grades; to arouse the curiosity of all children, and at the same time to cultivate their desire and capacity for inquiry; and to supply teachers with a variety of carefully thought-out and tested materials that they can use to build the elementary science curriculum best suited to the particular needs of their pupils.

The materials, published and distributed by the McGraw-Hill Book Company, consist of self-contained units, each built around a phenomenon a child can observe. Since learning theorists as yet cannot tell just which approach and experience, and in which sequence, will produce a condition to which a child responds, ESS materials offer situations conducive to the traditional and rational as well as to the intuitive and more playful learning approach.

Growing Seeds is recommended for children in kindergarten through 3rd grade; it introduces them to the characteristics of seeds and the use of informal measuring and graphing techniques. *Small Things,* designed for 4th to 6th graders, encourages children to use the microscope and examine familiar objects such as dust, an onion, hair, etc. Children devise units of measurement for their microscopic materials, sketch what they see, and start to generalize information about cells, living things, and non-living things. *The Behavior of Mealworms* presents 6th graders with an opportunity to learn about animal behavior patterns by letting them watch a simple organism. As questions are raised, experiments are devised to answer the questions. *Gases and Airs* is characterized as a laboratory investigation that teaches an area of science as well as a scientific approach. No particular style of teaching is called for and lessons are based on the assumption that children make discoveries, formulate hypotheses, and design experiments to test these hypotheses. An analysis of different "airs" and the measurement of air pressure form the core of this unit, which has been written for students between the 5th and 8th grades. The same grade levels are recommended for *Kitchen Physics,* although 3rd graders too enjoy many of its activities. This unit deals primarily with the properties of liquids. Children observe tension, adhesion, and viscosity but are encouraged to explain these concepts in words more common to their vocabulary; "grabbiness," "stickiness," and "holding together" are examples of acceptable expressions.

Several other units have been published in an experimental edition but will undergo further testing and revising before being released for final publication and distribution. Units usually consist of teachers' guides, equipment for children's use, work sheets to guide investigation, and such supplementary learning aids as films, film loops, and information booklets. Materials are tested, revised, and retested in more than 1,300 classrooms in urban, rural, and suburban schools; in wealthy and impoverished communities; and with children of greatly varying ages, interests, attitudes, skills, and backgrounds. Some eighty units are in various stages of development and the over-all plan foresees the production of between 100 and 200 units over the next ten years. Because of the program's experimental nature, sales of trial teaching materials remain subject to the project's control, but the first five units will be available from McGraw-Hill by the fall of 1966.

Members of the Elementary Science Study are well aware of the importance of teacher education. Considerable experimentation and research have shown that arranging for teachers to work with the new materials much as children would is one of the most effective methods of teacher preparation. In addition, ESS has made use of workshops, summer institutes, colloquia, meetings, and seminars to familiarize teachers with its products and to assist them in developing new attitudes toward children's learning. Cooperation with the Massachusetts State Teachers College system provides pre-service training to a small number of teachers, as does close association and integration with several schools of education.

Teachers who use ESS units experimentally are asked to submit periodic reports on their effectiveness with children; these comments and reactions are utilized in the revision of the units. Extensive evaluation in terms of trial teaching constitutes part of the project's testing program, and plans are being made to develop a more objective testing instrument for the project's materials.

Science—A Process Approach

During the summer of 1963 a writing group under the Commission on Science Education of the American Association for the Advancement of Science prepared a teachers' manual and a number of course content outlines in science for the early years of elementary schooling. Subsequent writing sessions extended the range of materials through grade 6. A revised edition of the content outlines has appeared in seven paper-back sections. The effort is being financed by grants from the National Science Foundation.

The fundamental assumptions underlying the proposed courses are that science is much more than a simple encyclopedic collection of facts, and that children in the primary grades can benefit from acquiring certain basic skills and competencies essential to the learning of science. These competencies have been identified as follows: observation, classi-fication, recognition and use of space-time relations, recognition and use of numbers and number relations, measurement, communication, inference, and prediction. After the 4th grade the emphasis is on the teaching of integrative processes that are interdependent to a certain degree. Children learn to make operational definitions, interpret data, control variables, experiment, and formulate hypotheses and models. The expectation is that the ability to use scientific processes will remain after many of the details of science have been forgotten. These com-petencies are advocated as appropriate for virtually all levels of science education and are not confined to the primary grades.

Four major areas of content, designated as appropriate for the first ten years of school, give some guidance in the selection of specific topics through which scientific behavior is to be achieved. These topics are:

• The universe—its galaxies, the solar system, the earth and the im-mediate environment, and measurements used to describe astronomical and geological phenomena.

• The structure and reactions of matter—compounds and mixtures, large and small molecules, elements, atoms, protons, neutrons, and electrons.

• The conservation and transformation of energy—the electromag-netic spectrum, motion and potential energy, electrical energy and chemical energy, force and work, and gravitational and magnetic fields.

• The interaction between living things and their environment—ani-mal and human behavior, the relation between biological structure and function, reproduction, development, genetics, evolution, and the bio-logical units of cell, organism, and population.

All of the books currently available are for teachers. The teachers' guide is an over-all view of the rationale of curriculum organization, of the subject matter, and of recommended instructional procedures. The other books outline the specific content and activities to be used by the teacher. Each of them lists a dozen or more topics, organized so as to remind the reader that they be used in developing student ability to observe, measure, classify, and communicate. Each topic is designed with two or three particular objectives in mind. Thus one of the topics of the first book, "Recognizing Regular Shapes," specifically states that upon completion of instruction the children should be able to recognize common two-dimensional shapes and to identify common shapes as components of complex objects.

At the end of each topic, ways are suggested to evaluate whether these aims have been achieved. This procedure is followed for all the topics covered by the booklets.

Experimental materials are currently being used by some 250 teachers in ten or more states. The project plans to revise each exercise three times and to test each revision in all its fourteen tryout centers. Under this plan, a completely revised K-6 curriculum would be available at the end of 1967.

This project recognizes the difficulties involved in choosing among sciences at the elementary-school level. Its current position is that no single science discipline should prevail, but that topics from many sciences and from mathematics should be woven into a unified whole; the goal is the development of basic scientific behavior in the student.

The advice to teachers to begin with Part One in the first grade (if there is no kindergarten), Part Two in the second grade, Part Three in the third grade, etc., raises some questions about how individual differences are to be handled. However, the project supplies a check list to help teachers determine pupil accomplishment so that they can adjust their teaching accordingly. How subsequent individualization of instruction is to be provided is not made clear, but it is anticipated that the feedbacks from trial use will influence the adjustments for differences in ability. In the final edition of *Science—A Process Approach*, the teacher will be given choices of exercises and sequences at each grade level.

Social Sciences

Curriculum building in the social studies might well be described as being in flux and confused. The general criticism during more than a decade has been that both the rigor of the social science disciplines and the unity of social science have been sacrificed to the amorphous studies of man and society or, worse, to the curricula in "social living" and "life adjustment."

More new projects are now appearing each year in the social sciences than in any other division of knowledge. It is difficult, therefore, to describe a fair cross section or to discern trends. Most of the new curricula seek to emphasize the concepts, principles, and methods of the social science disciplines. They stress the inductive method of learning; and such previously neglected social sciences as anthropology, economics, geography, political science, and sociology are receiving more attention than in the past. Even psychology is being considered as a potential subject for the schools.

The problems of choosing and combining fields, characteristic of curriculum planning in the natural sciences, are compounded in the social sciences. Only history holds a dominant position in the elementary-school program and is also represented in at least three years of the high-school curriculum. But even this discipline does not have a single project which has the visibility and the impact that SMSG has had in mathematics, PSSC in physics, and BSCS in biology.

Traditionally, history teachers have employed a chronological approach and students have been inundated by a flood of dates. New approaches, however, seek to develop a few historical events and epochs in depth (for example, the "postholing" approach of the ESI 10th-grade program); to identify concepts and structures of the social science disciplines (Edith West at Minnesota and Roy Price at Syracuse); to develop teaching strategies (notably the history project at Amherst); and to take students beyond the narrow parochialism of a Western viewpoint (the world history project at Northwestern University). We see throughout these projects, as with the natural sciences, an effort to replace "coverage" with an understanding of unifying concepts and competence in appropriate scientific methodologies.

Until recently curriculum building in the social sciences suffered from a serious shortage of funds; only a few of the disciplines qualified for National Science Foundation grants. Thus, when the Office of Education began to finance a Social Studies Program, it stimulated diverse and often pioneering activity. Much of the material is still in the process of development and not yet generally available.

Professional organizations and societies also have begun to sponsor projects; witness, for example, the work of the Joint Council on Economic Education and of the Association of American Geographers. Collaboration among groups is noteworthy. The Joint Committee on Civic Education (launched in 1964), for instance, involves the participation of the Lincoln Filene Center at Tufts, of UCLA, of the University of Michigan, and of the National Council for the Social Studies. The Lincoln Filene Center is preparing a content analysis of materials in civic education; UCLA has developed a unit in due process of law at its University Elementary School, and is testing it in neighboring schools; the University of Michigan is conducting a study of the political thinking of high-school students; and the NCSS is surveying promising curricular practices in civic education. The above is only a partial listing of committee activities but it illustrates the fresh interest in citizenship education.

The succeeding reports are designed to add some specificity to the foregoing synopsis. They leave no doubt that the whole range of the social studies program in the schools is being subjected to inquiry: objectives, sequences, materials, teaching and learning strategies, and evaluation, but a more penetrating analysis will have to await the developments of the next few years.

Social Studies Program in Research

The Social Studies Program was launched by the U.S. Office of Education in 1962 to improve instruction, research, and teacher education in the social sciences and to disseminate information. To implement these goals, the office, through its Cooperative Research Program, invited colleges, universities, and state departments of education to submit proposals for funds to conduct basic and applied research, to design activities that would stimulate research in the social science fields, and to establish curriculum development centers. In addition to other research, fourteen major curriculum projects were initiated, all of them sharing a commitment to these four objectives: 1) to redefine the scope and goals of the social studies curriculum; 2) to develop techniques and materials to achieve these goals; 3) to submit newly created materials to a sequence of experimentation, evaluation, and revision; 4) to disseminate the materials and relevant information.

The centers have certain features in common: They are located at universities and are headed by professors. They seek to identify the structure of social science disciplines and to develop new curricula around social science concepts. They involve the collaboration of university scholars with public-school teachers. They usually employ a set of teaching and learning techniques referred to as the inductive method or the inquiry approach. They emphasize the importance of critical thinking and of sequential and cumulative learning experiences. They are compiling many new materials and, using a multi-media approach, a variety of audio-visual aids. They try out new materials in classrooms of cooperating school systems, and are developing evaluative procedures.

The following projects, most of them five-year programs, are among those furthest along in the development of their materials. They are located at the following institutions:

Carnegie Institute of Technology. Edwin Fenton and John M. Good are directing the development of a new curriculum in history and the social sciences for able students in grades 9-12. All four courses will emphasize inductive methods, and materials are selected and prepared with this objective in mind. Two 9th-grade and two 10th-grade courses are ready for release into the public domain, and it is expected that the other sequences will follow at half-year intervals.

University of Minnesota. Under the direction of Edith West, this center is preparing and evaluating guides and materials for an articulated curriculum in grades K-14. No materials are available as yet.

Harvard University. Donald W. Oliver is directing a curriculum-development program based on the analysis of public controversy. Its objective is to train students to examine and analyze—through intensive debate and discussion—the kinds of disputes that give rise to social conflicts, and, by encouraging them to consider situations and problems in the light of social science concepts and theories, to aid them in discussing the value dilemmas on which controversy feeds.

Instructional materials consist primarily of case studies in a variety of forms: narrative accounts of events and people; newspaper reports; excerpts from novels; legal arguments; court decisions; historical vignettes, etc. They are designed to present the student with the concrete, raw data of human experience. The social science and analytic concepts are introduced by the teacher via the dialogue method.

The three-year sequence has been taught for nearly two years to a group of average-ability 10th-graders in a public high school in the Boston area, where trial teaching will continue for another year. An experimental edition of materials for students has been produced and a teachers' manual is in the discussion stage. Materials will be made available to teachers who want to try them out. The philosophy underlying this project is discussed in a recent publication by Donald W. Oliver and James P. Shaver, called *Teaching Public Issues in the High School,* and available from Houghton Mifflin in Boston.

Syracuse University. The purposes of this program are: to identify the major social science concepts and methodological tools that should be available to students in grades 5, 8, and 11; to examine how the social sciences and allied disciplines work; and to prepare illustrative materials for use by teachers and students that translate social science concepts and procedures into classroom practice. Instructional materials are still in the process of development. The director of the center is Roy A. Price, co-author with Warren Hickman and Gerald Smith of *Major Concepts for Social Studies,* a recent publication that is being distributed by the curriculum center.

University of Illinois. Ella Leppert directs a program that is concerned with the development of a three-year sequential junior-senior high-school curriculum that is to be part of a five-year sequence, designed to help students understand the basic structure of the social order, the dynamic nature of societies, and the effect of social change. Materials are in various stages of tryout.

Ohio State University. This center, under the direction of Meno Lovenstein, is developing 9th-grade curriculum materials for a semester course "based upon economics as a discipline." The plan is to provide teachers with a sequenced outline of the basic conceptual structure of economics. A teachers' guide and students' materials, consisting primarily of written dialogues, case studies, games and selected readings, are partially completed and not yet ready for distribution.

Amherst University. Richard H. Brown directs a curriculum development program to teach American history in junior and senior high schools using the inquiry approach. The staff prepares units primarily from source materials that deal with a period or topic in American history. Each unit contains materials for about two weeks' work. Eventually a short text will be written to link the individual units.

University of Georgia. Directed by Wilfred Bailey and Marion J. Rice, this program is producing anthropological units for use in social studies courses in grades 1-7. Staff members have selected appropriate content from the field, developed materials, trained teachers to use the materials, and tested some of the lessons in the classroom. Samples of pupils' materials and teachers' guides can be secured from the project.

The Social Studies Program expects to support additional centers and to continue the funding of research programs, large and small.

Social Studies Curriculum Program

The Social Studies Curriculum Program of Educational Services Incorporated was conceived at a two-week meeting in June, 1962, attended by some forty scholars from a wide variety of disciplines and several teachers. It was convened to explore the possibilities of extensive curriculum revision in the social studies and the humanities. (The project title originally included "and Humanities," which has since been dropped.)

There was general agreement that a large-scale effort to build at least a model of a new kind of curriculum for the social sciences and the humanities was urgently needed. There was further agreement that a radical revision of content, to be effective, had to be accompanied by an equally radical revision of the methods by which children are taught.

The new methodology, now generally referred to as the inductive method, would be based largely upon the goals and methodologies put forth some years earlier by Jerome S. Bruner in his influential book, *The Process of Education.*

Though the program would concern itself with grades K-12, the objective was not to develop a complete social studies curriculum, but rather to create model units and sequences for different levels of instruction and to demonstrate how to assemble given sequences so as to encourage others to arrange sequences to suit individual needs.

After the first year it became apparent that it was neither wise nor feasible to attempt to write large segments of a K-12 curriculum all at once, and the three divisions (elementary, junior high and senior high), therefore, began to concentrate their energies on small units or parts of units, intending to test these on children before starting to work on larger units or even courses.

The elementary-school division is now focusing its efforts on a general 5th-grade level unit that will combine into one experimental course the various parts of the elementary sequence as it was originally planned. The central theme is "Man" and children will study how five "great humanizing forces"—language, technology, social organization, child-rearing practices, and man's efforts to explain his world—have influenced his development. The elementary division has produced several films and some experimental material in mimeographed form.

The basic orientation of the junior high-school course is political. The theme, "Man and Politics," serves as a basis for the selection and treatment of material. Political science concepts such as power and political culture are used to organize the curriculum.

Staff members take care to explain that "Man and Politics" is an interdisciplinary sequence, involving political science, anthropology, and sociology, which focuses primarily on political ideas, values, and actions. It provides students with data that will assist them to develop concepts in their own terms, without being swamped by technical jargon. Models of instruction and content represent several alternatives to teachers and curriculum builders, and any one of the courses, or units within them, can be taught separately and independently of other courses or units.

"Inventing the Western World," the first course in a three-year sequence, treats the time span from 500 B.C. to 1600 A.D., and will present relevant case studies from the ancient and medieval worlds. One unit, dealing with the decline of the Roman republic, has been completed.

The 8th-grade course, labeled "From Subject to Citizen," has the pivotal position in the sequence. It consists of six units and treats selected periods of English and American history, beginning with "Elizabethan Society" and closing with a unit on the "American Constitution." The various units are in different stages of development and field testing; "The Emergence of the American," which draws its material from the Colonial Period of America (unit IV), has been published experimentally and is currently being used in some 250 classrooms in various parts of the country.

Content material for the last of the three courses of the junior high-school curriculum, tentatively entitled "The Civic Culture," is still being discussed. As planned at present, it will stress the study of such concepts as role, class, stereotype, etc., helping the student to become increasingly sophisticated in his use of conceptual tools.

The senior high-school program also consists of three courses, each at a different stage of development. Students in the first year of this sequence will study the impact of technology and science in the nineteenth and twentieth centuries. Units on the steam engine, the city of Manchester, and on scientific and social Darwinism have been tried out. This is to be followed in the 11th grade by an analysis of the relationship between ideology and reality in those centuries. The outline for the 12th-grade course calls for materials that will involve the student in a historical study of the social science disciplines, but it has not progressed beyond the research stage.

The Social Studies Curriculum has been supported by the National Science Foundation, the Ford Foundation, the Carnegie Corporation, and various other private philanthropic foundations. Typical of studies of this kind, it uses the discovery method and employs a broad range of instructional materials, including films, still pictures, loops, original documents, exercises and games, and kits of artifacts.

In addition, the program shares with other development projects the team approach to the improvement of the social science curriculum. Its large staff consists of scholars and teachers from many different disciplines, administrators, and educators, and is frequently augmented by painters, actors, dancers, and other artists who serve on a consultant basis. The creation of new materials and models calls for the cooperation of all of them.

Greater Cleveland Social Science Program

The Educational Research Council of Greater Cleveland, the parent organization of the Greater Cleveland Social Science Program, was created in 1959 as an independent, nonprofit and research organization to construct improved programs for use in kindergarten and the elementary and secondary schools. Impressed by the apparent need for a new mathematics curriculum, the council first sponsored a mathematics project (see page 26), and subsequently turned its attention to the social sciences.

Initiated in 1961, the council's social science project is attempting to develop a new curriculum characterized by the following features: sequential and cumulative development of goals and objectives, articulation of content to ensure continuous advancement of learning, and unity of purpose. Efforts have been made to include concepts and generalizations from such social science disciplines as history, geography, philosophy, economics, political science, psychology, sociology, and anthropology, and to give each discipline proportional consideration in the total curriculum.

In general terms, courses for grades K-3 lead the child to an understanding of an organized and functioning society and of his relationship to it; materials for grades 4-7 familiarize the student with some of the basic social science concepts and expand his knowledge of the world; and lessons for grades 8-12 deal, respectively, with: American history (8), comparative economic and political systems (9), international politics and economics, and a review of world history (10), economics and sociology (11), and American constitutional government and its historical development (12). Time for independent research and discussions has been included in the schedule of the last four years.

The program for grades K-4 has been completed. The text for grade 5 is being revised, and that for grade 6 will be introduced in the schools this year. Experimental units for grades 7, 8, and 9 will be tested during the 1966-67 school year. Material for grades 10-12 is still in outline form but public school districts wanting to reconstruct their social science curriculum have been provided with recommendations for an interim program.

A recently published two-part handbook assists teachers and administrators in the implementation of the new curriculum and also serves as a partial text for in-service education. A series of twelve telelecture tapes featuring outstanding speakers was prepared last year. These tapes, accompanied by manuals for administrators and teachers, are designed to increase the classroom teachers' knowledge of the social science disciplines.

The Greater Cleveland Social Science Program is currently being used by some 90,000 students in the participating schools of eighteen public school systems in the Cleveland area, two parochial school systems, two private schools, and five council school districts outside the Greater Cleveland area. Eleven non-council school districts are using the program on an experimental basis.

High-School Geography Project

The High-School Geography Project began in 1961 under the sponsorship of the Joint Committee on Education of the Association of American Geographers and the National Council for Geographic Education. Financial support for the project has come from the Fund for the Advancement of Education and in later years from the National Science Foundation.

From the beginning, work in the project differed in several aspects from that of other projects seeking to define the content of the high-school curriculum. Initiators of reform in physics, chemistry, biology, and mathematics, for example, could assume firm positions in the curriculum for their fields and begin immediately to redefine content and to formulate new approaches to teaching and learning. Geographers, however, could not assume a clear-cut position for geography in the social studies curriculum, let alone the establishment of a separate academic discipline to parallel the natural science disciplines.

During the first year, therefore, professional geographers prepared position papers seeking to define the place of geography in the schools, and the kind of course or courses that should prevail. A general Advisory Paper was subsequently published, outlining the objectives of geographic education, describing the general nature of the field of geography, and making recommendations on learning units. In the second year consideration was given to the testing of new methods and resource materials that had been developed by secondary-school teachers under the guidance of professional geographers. The teachers' experience was summarized in two documents: the HSGP Response Paper, and Selected Classroom Experiences: High School Geography Project. The third year was spent constructing two instructional units and preparing conceptual materials. School trials for these units began in 1965, and are now being conducted in seventy-five schools located in eleven states. Educational Testing Services, Inc. is assisting the project in an intensive evaluation of these materials.

According to Nicholas Helburn, project director since 1964, staff members will concentrate their future efforts on the completion of a ten-unit Settlement Theme course. After an introductory unit, the course offers two units on urban geography; two units on manufacturing and commercial agriculture, which introduce the student to economic geography; and a unit on cultural change that treats the diffusion of culture. Then, three units are designed to stretch the student's field of vision to include the uninhabited areas of the world, teach him the advantages or disadvantages of a given element (water), and stress the impact of political processes on settlement with human occupancy as a unifying theme. A unit on Japan allows the teacher to bring many of the previously introduced concepts together in a regional synthesis. A concluding unit will identify the frontier, i.e., some of the unsolved problems of modern geography.

Plans for the future include two reference volumes and the writing of additional course outlines dealing with regional geography, social problems, political geography, historical geography, and world patterns and processes.

Anthropology Curriculum Study Project

The Anthropology Curriculum Study Project, sponsored by the American Anthropological Association and supported financially by the National Science Foundation, was established in 1962 to explore the status and potentialities of anthropology for the high-school curriculum. Headquarters are at 5632 Kimbark Avenue, Chicago; Malcolm Collier is project director.

The place of anthropology in the high-school curriculum is somewhat similar to that of geography. Both are implicitly a part of the curriculum in the social studies; geography, however, is more frequently taught in high school as a separate course. Anthropology enters into the humanities and biology, just as geography runs through several phases of the natural sciences. Neither, however, has a firm place as a separate discipline.

The principal tasks of the project have been to define the role of anthropology in the high-school curriculum, to identify the anthropological data and concepts that are important to secondary education, and to develop useful and practical ways of introducing anthropological substance and concepts into the high-school classroom.

As in so many other projects, the preparation of materials is seen as one of the means to these ends. The topics presented include subjects which anthropologists consider most relevant to high-school studies and in which they are specialists. The materials include readings, plastic reproductions of bones and tools, slides and slide-tapes, overhead transparencies, and evidence cards. All this is being prepared by anthropologists after extensive discussion of the topics with high-school teachers. Teachers' guides accompany each unit. The intent of the project is not to create a separate high-school course in anthropology. Instead, the major use of the material will be in history courses and perhaps in introductory social studies units in the early high-school years. Considerable teaching flexibility has been achieved by preparing the content in booklet form.

Materials in experimental use include the "Study of Early Man," a unit on biocultural evolution, and "The Great Transformation," a booklet describing the changes experienced by man following the domestication of animals and plants. Both texts are being tested in a number of schools, and revision, incorporating more than two years of classroom experience, is currently under way.

In various stages of development are units to acquaint students with the use and application of social science concepts, and area studies of Africa, Latin America, and the Middle East.

Two American Indian case studies—*The Great Tree and the Long-house: the Culture of the Iroquois,* and *Kiowa Years*—are being published by Macmillan; they are accompanied by teachers' guides that suggest a variety of classroom uses for the materials. Material to be published late this year includes *The Idea of Liberty in American Culture* by R. Hanvey, and *An Annotated Bibliography of Anthropological Materials for Secondary School Use.*

Initial reports suggest a growing enthusiasm among high-school teachers at the prospect of infusing the social science curriculum with concepts and methodology derived from anthropology.

The Developmental Economic Education Program

As the curriculum reform in the social studies is gaining momentum, economics seems to be emerging as a discipline that will be represented in the schools through many different projects. Economics also seems to be attracting a large number of able and qualified scholars, who are devoting a great deal of time and effort to update their discipline's subject matter. The lack of government funding, until very recently, has partly been compensated by financial support from the business community.

The new curricula in economics generally echo the basic objectives of the multidiscipline social studies projects. Most economic programs fall into one of two categories: they consider economics qua economics, or treat it as it relates to another discipline—for instance, a course in civics or in American or world history. Economists have increasingly emphasized the importance of acquainting the student with economics thinking, and have stressed the discipline's relevance to historical events and periods. They have come to realize that the picture of economics as it appears in the conventional American history textbook is badly distorted, and have therefore begun to create separate economics units for certain periods in history—the Jacksonian age, for example—that can be used in conjunction with existing textbook materials.

One of the major programs in economics education is the Developmental Economic Education Program (DEEP), started in 1964 by the Joint Council on Economic Education (JCEE). The council is a non-profit, independent, educational organization, which has been supported by funds from business, labor, agriculture, and philanthropic institutions, and lately from the National Science Foundation and the Office of Education. Its goals include increasing the understanding of economics and the use of improved methods and materials in teaching this discipline.

DEEP is an action program designed to develop materials for grades K-12. It is concerned primarily with rebuilding the curriculum at the local level and thus encourages schools in participating city and county systems to construct and test their own sequences. Pilot schools are assisted by a part-time or full-time DEEP coordinator (usually a teacher) and a university-trained economist. A two-part JCEE publication, *Teachers Guide to the Developmental Economic Education Program,* serves as a guide and is available from the Joint Council. Part I outlines the ideas and concepts which are considered essential in the understanding of economics; Part II contains suggestions for their development and indicates by grouped grade levels the placement of economics ideas. Concepts are arranged in a spiraling fashion and are repeated at increasingly higher levels of understanding.

Schools receive some financial support from the JCEE, but a considerable amount of aid comes from local sources and school systems. The council expects that some thirty school systems will be involved with DEEP by 1967; projects last three years.

In addition to DEEP, the Joint Council in conjunction with the forty-four affiliated state and regional councils supports a variety of secondary-school projects. Teacher education is another of the council's concerns. College courses, TV lessons, workshops, summer institutes, films, and field personnel have all been used to increase teachers' understanding of economics. Both pre-service and in-service education have received a good deal of attention.

Elkhart Experiment
in Economic Education

The Elkhart (Indiana) Experiment in Economic Education is another K-12 economics program, set up in 1958 by Lawrence Senesh of Purdue University. Funded by the university, the Elkhart Public Schools, the Carnegie Corporation, and other interested organizations, the new curriculum is based on the assumption that children can grasp an abstract idea if it forms a part of their own experiences, and that such ideas can be presented in a way that reflects the basic structure of economic knowledge.

The project does not deal exclusively with economics but includes such other areas of social studies as geography, history, political science, sociology, and anthropology.

Materials are now available for grades 1-3, and are called, respectively, "My Home," "My Neighborhood," and "The City." The unit for grade 4 is being trial-taught in the cooperating schools, and work for grade 5 is still in the planning stage. (Science Research Associates in Chicago publishes and distributes the materials.)

Some of the new lessons will be used by 160,000 first- and second-graders in the New York City school system this fall. Children will begin by listing what they would like to own and what it would cost, quickly discovering the all too familiar conflict between expanding wants and limited means.

Marginal utility and other basic economic principles are presented in a similarly practical manner.

Senesh and his associates in the project look upon the existing units as resource aids. These units consist of a teachers' guide with lesson plans, films, and a series of recordings that constitute the heart of the lesson. The lessons are designed to last from one week to several weeks, and teachers are encouraged to choose from a variety of activities those that will best fit their group and get across the ideas of the lesson. An annotated bibliography of relevant books and filmstrips concludes each lesson plan.

Evaluation and teacher training, pre-service as well as in-service, will receive increasing attention in the coming years.

Sociological Resources for Secondary Schools

Sociological Resources for Secondary Schools is an official project of the American Sociological Association. It was established in 1964 at Dartmouth College in Hanover, New Hampshire, and is being supported with funds from the National Science Foundation. In September, 1966, Robert A. Feldmesser, professor of sociology at Dartmouth, was succeeded as director by Robert C. Angell, professor at the University of Michigan, where the project will now be located.

The major goal of SRSS, as stated in its prospectus, is to develop high-quality instructional materials that will reflect sociology as a scientific discipline and that will be suitable for use in secondary-school courses in sociology, history, problems of democracy, and other subjects. Efforts will be made to incorporate the cumulative findings of modern research and to upgrade the substantive and methodological materials available to social studies teachers.

Subject matter will be presented through a series of units (termed episodes) that will examine specific subjects, such as population; urbanism; stratification and mobility; the impact of science and technology on family, education, religion; and other aspects of present-day existence. Teams of sociologists and collaborating social studies teachers select and organize content material. Each episode is complete in itself and occupies approximately ten hours of classroom time.

By mid-1966, thirty units were in various stages of development; some were being evaluated; some were undergoing their first, second, or third revision; and some were being tested in cooperating schools. All contained a combination of the following items: a statement of the problem; introductory material indicating the significance of the problem to the student and to the problems he will deal with as an individual and a member of society; instructions to the student for collecting and processing data; descriptive, historical, or summarizing statements; questions for discussion or contemplation; and suggestions for additional reading by the student as well as the teacher. As planned at present, the first of the project's materials, i.e., texts, teachers' manuals, exercises, tests, films, etc., will be made available in the fall of 1967; completion of the publication program is not expected until 1970.

Humanities

The 1964 report on the changing curriculum, *School Curriculum Reform in the United States,* identified curricular imbalance as a major agenda item for the near future. The problem then was the absence of curriculum activity in the humanities, particularly in the arts, apparently due in part to the lack of funds. This imbalance still exists. There are promising signs, however, that steps to correct it are under way.

Although public discontent with the state of mathematics and the natural sciences in the high schools became known early in the 1950's, curricular reform in these fields remained embryonic until 1957 and several years thereafter. Serious, reasonably organized dialogue regarding the humanities did not begin until the late 1950's and early 1960's. (Modern foreign languages fared somewhat better.) In other words, the school curriculum reform in most humanistic disciplines lags behind that in mathematics and the natural sciences by about a decade. And without an occurrence in the humanities equivalent to that of Sputnik, the gap may well increase.

At times it seems as though certain forces and factors in modern America are conspiring against a greater emphasis on the humanities in elementary and secondary education. For example, we are constantly reminded of the need to prepare ourselves to live effectively in a technological society that confounds our comprehension. But instead of drawing on the humanistic disciplines for help we act as though the future will require only scientific insight—a conclusion that may be quite faulty. We live, furthermore, in a period when the need for humanitarian action rather than humanistic inquiry appears to be urgent.

In most schools, literary and artistic pursuits are still on the fringes of pre-collegiate academic life. To quote Martin Bernheimer, "Unless we do something quickly, our children will be culturally deprived because they are educationally deprived."[13]

There is evidence that some real efforts are being made to revise the teaching of English and modern foreign languages. But we still do not

---

13. Martin Bernheimer, "Music Depreciation in Our Public Schools," *Los Angeles Times* (Calendar Section), June 12, 1966.

accord foreign languages the position in the school curriculum that is commensurate with their importance, and we treat the arts as though they were an extracurricular luxury.

The English Program

Project English, now known as the English Program of the U.S. Office of Education, was initiated in the fall of 1961 to bring about improved instruction at all levels in English literature, reading, and writing; to coordinate the efforts of teachers, university scholars, and school administrators in improving the quality of English teaching; to assist universities in the establishment of centers for the development of new curriculum materials and teaching methods; to sponsor research and experimentation; and eventually to disseminate the new knowledge gained from these endeavors.

Since its inception the project has supported some 120 research studies, which have been concerned primarily with the problems relating to reading, language, composition and connected skills, and have been concerned with all teaching levels—college, secondary, and elementary, including a few preschool investigations. The studies have dealt with such diverse subjects as the learning process and the factors affecting learning; the communication barriers of the culturally deprived; the types of sentence structures used by superior students and adults; and the advantages and disadvantages of programed learning materials. Roughly a third of the approved research projects have been completed, with work on the remaining two thirds still in progress.

More dramatic than the research effort, however, and of great potential benefit to the schools has been the establishment of twenty-five curriculum-study and demonstration centers, which, despite individual differences, have several characteristics in common. They are designed to develop sequential patterns for the teaching of reading, composition, and/or related language skills; to test promising practices and materials; and to recommend curricular innovations. The cooperation of departments of English and education and of several school systems is frequently a feature of the projects. Most of the centers deal with the secondary-school curriculum, except for two that are producing a K-12 sequence. Some have no materials as yet, others have not had a chance to test them. Furthest along are the six institutions that received their grants during the first year the English Program was in operation, 1962: Carnegie Institute of Technology, Northwestern University, University of Nebraska, Hunter College, University of Minnesota, and University of Oregon.

Using the inductive teaching method and an integrated, sequential and cumulative approach, *Carnegie Institute of Technology* has developed a curriculum for able college-bound students in grades 10-12. Although literature is at the core of the program, composition and language study are closely tied to it. Tenth-grade literature material deals primarily with the universal concerns of man as they appear in world literature; in the 11th grade the emphasis is on American literature and its reflections of American culture patterns from the time of the Puritans to the present; and 12th-grade students concentrate on English literature as exemplified in such literary art forms as the tale, the tragedy, the epic, the satire, etc. Literature accounts for approximately 50 percent of the new curriculum's class time, composition for 32 percent, and language study for 18 percent. This program has been completed and its materials are now available.

In 1964, furthermore, Carnegie began work on a related two-year program to see how useful the new materials may be for general 10th, 11th, and 12th-grade high-school students, and to determine also whether the course materials are written explicitly enough to be taught by teachers who have not had special training at the curriculum-study center.

The center at *Northwestern University* is constructing a curriculum for the teaching of English composition and has been preparing a number of lessons on the basic processes of composition in junior high school. New materials are tested in nine neighboring school systems.

One of the more ambitious programs is being conducted by the *University of Nebraska,* which has developed and tested new materials for language, literature, and composition classes from K-12. (The Nebraska project did not start as a federal project but received its grant from the English Program after a group of scholars and teachers, with support from a local foundation, had initiated work on a blueprint for a

K-12 curriculum that was to incorporate the best then known about the nature and teaching of English.)

The elementary-school program, consisting of sixty-six units, attempts to integrate composition and language with literature through the study of myths, comedies, romances, biographies, and other literary art forms. The center's junior high-school units begin with a literary or linguistic core and then move on to composition. The senior high-school curriculum involves the student in the study of persuasion, logic, and straight thinking, and guides him into using what he has learned about rhetoric, literary modes, and linguistic forms in the writing of his own compositions.

While the literature program makes up the bulk of the new materials at all levels, much of it is used to support, directly or indirectly, the composition and language programs.

Instructional units generally consist of packets for teacher and student, each containing reading materials, background information, and study questions. Tests conducted in nineteen schools in five districts indicate that the center's current program is most effective with bright children.

The center at *Hunter College* aims to select and evolve reading and language materials that will meet the special needs of junior high-school students from culturally deprived urban environments, and to develop methods and teaching guides for the pre-service and in-service training of the English teachers who instruct these students. The materials are built on the communication patterns of the children, and the methods take into consideration the middle-class values of teachers, which often make it difficult for them to understand the underprivileged student's learning difficulties. Since these students have been found to be particularly responsive to audio-visual aids, efforts are being made to train instructors in adapting those materials to the teaching of reading.

Units for grades 7-9 are being used experimentally in a number of New York City schools, where teachers receive special in-service training by means of video-taped English classes from special service schools and a series of manuals on increasing the motivation of slow and reluctant readers. Some of the materials will be commercially available by September, 1966; final dissemination is scheduled for 1967.

Minnesota University's curriculum center is using a somewhat different approach in preparing and evaluating a language-centered curriculum for grades 7-12. Secondary-school teachers and consultants have developed a set of resource materials that includes units on syntactic relationships, the dictionary, and transformational grammar, as well as items to test linguistic sensitivity. Four-fifths of the planned teaching units are completed, and a test to measure knowledge of language concepts is in the process of development.

The *University of Oregon* center, in cooperation with seven school systems, is directing its efforts toward improving the curriculum in language, literature, and rhetoric in grades 7-12 for all but the students of lowest ability. The language curriculum consists mainly of an inductive study of transformational grammar, supplemented by a study of the nature of language, the history of English dialects, phonology, and similar material. The literature curriculum is built around the three concepts of subject, form, and point of view, and focuses on the literary work itself rather than on literary periods or the biographies of authors.

Rhetorical theory provides the basis for the rhetoric curriculum and its subdivisions: substance, structure, and style. Also included is the study of semantics and logic with application to writing and speaking. Emphasis on speech is a noteworthy feature of this curriculum. A course taught in grade 11 affords the student a chance to study voice and speech with a qualified professional.

Among curriculum projects that received grants later, three are of a somewhat specialized nature:

Columbia University has organized a set of materials designed to teach English as a second language to children in the early elementary grades, and is trying out completed materials in schools on Indian reservations, as well as in New York City, Ethiopia, Peru, and Colombia.

Gallaudet College has developed improved methods and materials to teach English to deaf students at the college preparatory level. Aware of these students' peculiar ability for modern mathematics, program members are taking advantage of this strength by using mathematical symbols to express grammatical relationships and by designing materials that appeal primarily to the eye.

The curriculum study center at the *University of Illinois* is concentrating on the preparation of secondary-school English teachers, a project that involves the cooperative efforts of twenty representative Illinois colleges and universities. Each institution is developing a program appropriate to its resources and personnel so that the outcome will not be one but a number of improved programs. Undergraduate and graduate studies as well as upgrading the competency of currently employed teachers are among the project's major concerns.

In summary, curriculum centers are playing an important role in the efforts to redefine English as a subject of study in the schools, in instituting changes in the pre- and in-service education of teachers, and in pointing the way for the future. There is little doubt that the "new" English will be characterized by carefully structured curricula taught inductively; by literature courses that emphasize depth and analysis, and lead the student to appreciate literary craftsmanship and its relation to meaning; and by an interest in structural linguistics, in generative grammar, and in speech as an integral part of the curriculum.

Besides supporting studies in basic and applied research and curriculum centers, the English Program has also funded a number of demonstration centers, whose purpose it is to test new materials, methods, and techniques, and to publicize programs that have proved effective. Demonstrations make use of live classroom settings, ETV, radio, and other communication media. New York University, for instance, has prepared films demonstrating the teaching of linguistics in secondary schools. The University of California (Berkeley) has produced kinescopes to teach various literary genres to 10th graders. Western Reserve University has conducted workshops and conferences to display a junior high-school program in literature, language, and composition for average and honors students. Tuskegee Institute has undertaken to identify the problems of functional illiterates as they exist in a southern county as well as to test and evaluate several experimental teaching methods, the results to be used in the construction of an appropriate educational program.

Though the English Program is too young in terms of years to have brought about revolutionary changes, a number of results have begun to emerge. Educators and academicians are working toward a common goal in a new spirit of cooperation; expanding funds have been accompanied by an increasing number of innovative and imaginative proposals; the interest of academicians in disciplines other than English has been aroused; and future needs have been brought into sharper focus.

Summer institutes in English, supported with funds made available through the National Defense Education Act (NDEA), were started in 1965, under the auspices of the Office of Education. As has been the case all along, secondary-school education received considerably more attention than elementary schools. Of the 105 general and special institutes, only three were designed for elementary-school teachers. The number of institutes and participants has increased in 1966, and the distribution of subject-matter components for all levels of instruction was greatly improved.

The Commission on English

The Commission on English was established in September, 1959, as an autonomous body of the College Entrance Examination Board to encourage and facilitate a gradual nationwide improvement in curriculum, teacher training, and the methods of classroom instruction; to propose standards of achievement for students and suggest ways of meeting them; and to stimulate cooperative efforts between colleges and high schools to achieve these aims.

The commission's members, all teachers of English, spent several years investigating and examining secondary-school English and in 1965 published the results of their inquiry in a report called *Freedom and Discipline in English*. This document appeared at a time when English was taking on a new dimension. Congress had approved the establishment of a National Foundation on the Arts and the Humanities; textbook writers of English and their publishers were planning a greater number of books of the kinds that teachers really need; the federal government—through the Office of Education—was providing funds to support basic and applied research, publications, curriculum development, and, for the first time, a national program of summer institutes for advanced study for English teachers.

This favorable climate notwithstanding, the commission decided to concentrate its efforts on over-all improvement rather than on specific innovation. Its report, therefore, does not provide a curriculum for grades 9-12, and it does not contain a prescribed list of books for classroom and independent study. It does, however, demand greater competence in teaching, and insists on certain changes that will enable the teacher to do a better job. In addition to an analysis of the weaknesses and strengths of the current high-school English program, the report devotes a chapter each to language, literature, and composition—written for teachers and the trainers of teachers—and lists fourteen recommendations that, if adopted, would improve the quality of teaching.

Eight of these recommendations deal with teaching conditions, course load, pupil load, and class size. Four are concerned with professional standards and call for college and university English departments to assume a more vigorous role in the training of future elementary and secondary-school teachers. Curriculum is the subject of the remaining recommendations. The scope of the English program is defined as the study of language, literature, and composition (written and oral). The teacher is advised to disregard any matters not directly related to these subjects. The curriculum, the authors contend, should be the result of cooperative planning by all teachers involved in the study of English and should represent a clearly defined sequence from grade to grade.

While it is still too early to assess the long-range effects of the commission's report, there is no doubt that the book will constitute a valuable tool for teacher-training programs and will assist curriculum supervisors, faculty deans, teachers, administrators, and interested laymen in their efforts to discourage mediocrity and to reward excellence in the teaching of English. The patterns and proposals set forth in *Freedom and Discipline in English* have already proved useful in the organization of the NDEA institutes.

The commission's work, however, did not terminate with the report. The trustees of the College Board voted in 1964 to extend the operation of the commission's Boston office for at least three years; the commission continues to function as a clearinghouse and information center for matters pertaining to English and to provide consultant services for the Office of Education as well as for the educational community at large.

In August, 1965, the commission sponsored a two-week conference for summer institute directors and teachers because it felt that the report of past successes and failures of the NDEA institutes would be of value to future institutes. The directors and instructors were given some training and the opportunity to exchange information and share their experiences, thereby preventing waste of effort, time, and money through needless repetition.

The commission's kinescopes, made by master teachers and concerned with the basic problems in the teaching of English, continue to be in demand. Of the eleven films that have been completed, six deal with literature, four with composition, and one with modern linguistics. With the scripts now available separately, these films constitute an inexpensive and efficient way of bringing some of the best techniques of teaching to an ever growing number of secondary-school teachers. Production of a second series is now in progress.

It is through such activities and a variety of publications that the commission has tried to carry out what it was charged with initially by Frank Bowles, then president of the College Board: to determine the difference between what is achieved in secondary school and what is expected in college by way of competence in English, and to suggest how the difference is to be reduced to agreement.[14]

Modern Foreign Languages

We have chosen to present a general discussion of modern foreign languages rather than of individual projects, largely because the central stimulating force, the Modern Language Association, embraces several languages and an impressive array of activities. Most of what follows pertains to secondary education.

Twenty years ago, the teaching of modern foreign languages was at a low ebb, due partly to the fact that a course in a foreign language was generally considered an elective. To instruct elementary-school children in foreign languages was virtually unheard of, except for a handful of

---

14. Annual Report of the College Board, 1963-64, p. 49. New York: College Entrance Examination Board, 1964.

"prestige," private schools. Clearly, the changes that have taken place since then are impressive.

Prior to World War II, foreign language instructors in high schools concentrated on developing in their students the ability to read and write the language they were studying. During the war, however, members of the armed forces were instructed by teachers who used an audio-visual approach and who emphasized speaking, listening comprehension, and analysis of the structure of a language as well as reading and writing.

Efforts were made after the war to introduce this new approach in some schools but the notion that a foreign language could be learned during a two-year period of mostly reading-and-writing instruction in high school persisted until the early Fifties, when two events occurred that were instrumental in changing the status quo: the U.S. Commissioner of Education strongly recommended the teaching of foreign languages as a basic element of general education; and the Modern Language Association (MLA), supported by a grant from the Rockefeller Foundation, began an investigation of the place of foreign language in American education and life. The six-year inquiry resulted in recommendations that included the preparation of longer study sequences, installation of language laboratories, and increased use of such technological aids as tape recorders, film strips, and teaching machines, and culminated with the inclusion of a Language Development Program in the National Defense Education Act of 1958.

As early as 1953, MLA's Foreign Language Program (FLP) had begun to conduct workshops and conferences to discuss the content, teaching methods, and materials of a movement that favored teaching foreign languages in elementary schools (FLES). FLP generally endorsed the FLES program and sponsored the preparation of teachers' guides in French, German, and Spanish for use in grades 3-6. Other FLP activities included the publication of two policy statements—one dealing with the qualifications for secondary-school teachers of foreign languages, the other with the value of foreign language teaching—and a program of cooperation with many agencies and groups in the investigation and development of policies, plans, and materials for language teaching. Serving as a sponsor and clearinghouse for projects to improve the field, FLP has been a major force in the upgrading and expansion of foreign language instruction.

Since the basic idea of the audio-lingual approach has now been generally accepted by the profession, two-year language programs have increasingly been replaced by four- to nine-year programs. The A-LM materials (Audio-Lingual Materials), originally developed by the Modern Language Materials Center under a grant from NDEA, provide a six-year sequence for the teaching of French, German, Italian, Russian, and Spanish in grades 7-12. Available from Harcourt, Brace, & World, Inc., they, along with other materials, have become the model for writers of the newer modern language curricula that are now being produced by commercial publishers.

Audio and visual aids have become integral parts of the modern language teaching program. The number of language laboratories has grown from several dozen in 1957 to at least 8,000 in 1966, chiefly as a result of NDEA assistance. The support provisions of the recently enacted Elementary and Secondary Education Act of 1965 could give foreign language study an additional boost.

Two other developments in the field of foreign language teaching deserve mention: the introduction of the less commonly taught languages in elementary and secondary schools, and the teaching of subject matter in a foreign language.

NDEA has supported the preparation of materials for the teaching of the unusual languages in college, which should in time increase the supply of instructors qualified to teach these languages in the secondary school. Portuguese, Greek, and Hebrew are successfully being taught in public schools, as are Arabic, Chinese, and Japanese, for which carefully designed materials, using the audio-lingual approach, are available.

The teaching of other disciplines in a foreign language naturally presupposes a certain degree of language proficiency on the part of the student, and such projects are therefore usually found at the advanced levels of a six or nine-year modern language sequence. There are school systems that are teaching world history in French, German, and Spanish; Latin-American history in Spanish; and biology in German.

The development of new curricular materials necessitated the development of new tests, an area in which the Modern Language Association has been particularly active. Its Cooperative Foreign Language Tests, prepared in cooperation with the Educational Testing Service and with support from NDEA and the Office of Education, constitute a series of tests that measure a student's competence in the five most commonly taught languages: French, German, Italian, Russian, and Spanish. The tests provide separate measures of skills in listening, speaking, reading, and writing at two levels of achievement and may be purchased from the Educational Testing Service.

Curricular revisions often require the retraining of teachers, and the foreign language field is no exception. More than 500 summer and year-long modern language institutes have been conducted since the summer of 1959, when NDEA money first became available for this purpose. Approximately 27,000 teachers have been exposed to language courses offering additional training in the commonly taught languages, as well as in Arabic, Chinese, Japanese, modern Hebrew, and Italian. Teachers who have attended a first-level institute may enroll for advanced training institutes that are being held in Latin America, Germany, France, Russia, Spain, and Israel.

NDEA funds during the last seven years have also helped to finance more than 350 research and study projects designed to improve instruction in the modern foreign languages. By 1966, many colleges, universities, professional associations, and public school systems had participated in the development of specialized teaching materials and of more effective ways of teaching in over 125 different languages.

It is hoped that additional research in the psychology of language learning and preparation of basic materials in the uncommonly taught languages will, in the words of the Congress, "correct as rapidly as possible the existing imbalances . . . which have led to an insufficient proportion of our population educated in . . . modern foreign languages."

The Arts

The situation in the arts also lends itself better to a general discussion than to an analysis of specific projects. Although the status of the arts in the curricula of elementary and secondary education is still low, we can report some auspicious developments.

Teachers of fine and applied arts have fought a lonely battle to secure a foothold in the regular school curriculum and to maintain it. Sputnik did not help. As a matter of fact, there is ample evidence of budgetary and curricular erosions to make room for the increased emphasis on the so-called "hard-core" subjects.

Such art and music as are available in elementary schools are taught primarily by regular classroom teachers whose preparation usually consists of a single course in art education or music education, or sometimes in both. In the city of Los Angeles, for example, only one-fourth of the students receive instruction from a music specialist, and then only for an average of one twenty-five-minute period a week. Prosperous suburban communities do better; many school systems do worse. Dance and drama are almost nonexistent, except for a few elective courses at the secondary level. In fact, the small amount of instruction in the arts provided for elementary-school children ceases in the high schools and is replaced by drama clubs, orchestras, bands, and dance groups for the talented few. The arts simply are not an organized part of the general education of most public school students in the United States.

The government's increasing concern with the arts promises to change this situation—but the struggle will be long and uphill. The fight is being taken up by the newly created National Foundation in the Arts and the Humanities in Washington and by the Arts and Humanities Program of the Office of Education. Both newcomers are adding considerable strength to the traditional efforts of professional organizations and some private foundations. Art teachers are now turning their attention increasingly to the content of their courses and the methods of teaching them.

OE's Arts and Humanities Program was set up in 1964 "to help extend and improve education in the arts and humanities at all levels" and functions in much the same way as the English and the Social Studies Programs do, but on an as yet much smaller scale. In the beginning, research projects were funded through the Cooperative Research Act, but additional funds have recently become available and allocations have increased from $600,000 during the first year to $2,400,000 in 1966. On the assumption that planning in these content areas is the function of an educational laboratory, to be carried on outside of a school system as well as inside of it, the Office of Education is currently considering the establishment of R and D centers for the humanities and arts.

One of the first projects the program supported was a seminar at Yale devoted to the improvement of music education in elementary and secondary schools. In a workshop-like manner, participants discussed, among other topics, the development of musicality, the broadening of the music repertory, and the importance of listening as a key to musical understanding. They also concerned themselves with teaching aids and teacher education, pre-service as well as in-service, and outlined some areas that are particularly suitable for educational research and development. The subsequently published report of the conference's proceedings gained significance because it was the first document that brought the problems of music education to the nation's attention.

Another milestone in curriculum development in music education for elementary and secondary schools was the establishment of the Contemporary Music Project, sponsored by the Music Educators National Conference in 1963. CMP has supported workshops in contemporary music and assisted experimental projects in various schools to explore teaching techniques through creative approaches. Observations gained during the administration of these projects and in visits and consultations with music faculties and administrators have been evaluated and are now being used to update the music education of teachers.

An OE-supported three-year project at the Juilliard School of Music in New York has resulted in the creation of an enlarged music repertory for grades K-6. The new anthology is currently being tested in six selected school systems, and should be commercially available soon.

By July, 1966, the Arts and Humanities Program had supported forty-six educational research projects in art, six in museum education, forty-eight in music, eighteen in theatre and dance, four in the arts in general, and eleven in the humanities.

The summer of 1966 marked the beginning of NDEA summer institutes for music teachers, and it is hoped that institutes for teachers of other artistic endeavors will follow soon.

These are encouraging signs, but much more effort is needed if the place and the teaching of the arts in our schools are to change soon and significantly.

Health Education

Health has never been a clearly defined study in our schools. At the elementary level it is frequently taught in combination with science but the impending reform in the sciences may well push it in to the secondary-school curriculum; in the high schools health is commonly combined with physical education and becomes the subject of discussion chiefly when inclement weather disrupts outdoor activities.

The project described below was chosen for presentation here because it illustrates a curricular approach that differs from that of most other projects.

School Health Education Study

The School Health Education Study was initiated in 1961 under the direction of Elena M. Sliepcevich, formerly professor of health education at Ohio State University. Its work had been supported by several grants from the Samuel Bronfman Foundation until, in 1966, it received a grant from the Minnesota Mining and Manufacturing Co. to continue the development and publication of curriculum materials. SHES operates out of the NEA's Washington offices.

Set up originally to examine the status and curriculum of health instruction in grades K-12, the project's scope was soon enlarged to include the development and testing of experimental curriculum materials. The results of the nationwide survey, published in a Summary Report, June, 1964, clearly showed health education's low status in the school curriculum, the insufficient study time allotted to it, and the students' alarming ignorance in matters of health. A background study revealed the major research needs in school health education.

Contrary to current curriculum projects which move into the production of their materials rather quickly, usually during the first summer after the initial committee meetings, the SHES first dealt with the problems of objectives, organization, and evaluation. As a consequence, initial documents define the field from a curricular point of view; designed for the teacher instead of the student, they justify and encourage the creation of several curricular alternatives.

Teaching guides state behavioral outcomes, content, and learning opportunities for each age level. Three key concepts provide the framework: growing and developing, decision making, and interaction. These, in turn, are broken down into ten major concepts that serve as organizing elements for thirty-one substantive points, called focal organizing elements. All curricular components have been developed in an ascending hierarchy, and the physical, mental, and social dimensions of each have been explicitly stated. The study thus exemplifies how the suggestions of a curriculum inquiry can be used successfully in developing a curricular guide. It is unfortunate that the terminology slowly gaining acceptance among curriculum theorists was not followed throughout, but this is a minor concern considering the consistency of the effort as a whole.

Experimental materials have been designed for four levels: lower elementary (K-3); upper elementary (4-6); junior high (7-9); and senior high (10-12). Working at first only with the concepts of decision making and interaction, staff members have created a teaching-learning guide for each concept and each level, with lists of resource aids for teachers and students. In addition to instructional materials, participating teachers receive supplementary materials, informing them about the use of concepts in learning and teaching and describing the principles of learning in general.

An evaluation plan has been developed to obtain data on teacher and student reaction, on pre- and post-test performance of students, and on the effectiveness of the teaching materials. Revisions are made on the basis of information provided by some twenty-five schools located in four tryout centers in California, Illinois, New York, and Washington. Revised units will be published over a three-year period, beginning at the end of 1966.

No attempt will be made to present the new sequence as a national curriculum. Health-education specialists, classroom teachers, and supervisors who collaborated in constructing the sequence, view it as an outline that local school systems can utilize in preparing health-education curricula best suited to their particular needs. Instructors who have begun to use the materials report that elementary-school children seem enthusiastic over the solid material they are now getting in the field of health education.

Related Educational Programs and Activities

The foregoing descriptions of projects and activities in various subject fields cover a representative sample of current curriculum reform in the United States. They are proof of the steadily increasing interest in improving the curriculum by constructing new courses and producing more effective teaching materials. The many other curricular and instructional efforts—too numerous to be included here—are additional evidence of the intense efforts on the part of educators and laymen to raise the quality of American education.

Curriculum planning by local school districts, so characteristic of the period immediately following World War II, has not ceased. Curriculum guides are still being exchanged between county, city, and suburban school systems, and materials prepared locally have a strong influence on school practices at both elementary and secondary levels.[15] Usually, these guides list a wide assortment of learning resources that teachers may use: notably, films, filmstrips, supplementary texts, paperback books, and records.

Publishers such as the McGraw-Hill Book Company and the Encyclopaedia Britannica Educational Corporation prepare and distribute a wide assortment of films and film strips, many of them first-rate. Unfortunately, neither the teaching profession nor the school buildings are equipped to make the most of these newer instructional media. Relatively few teachers are aware of the vast opportunities for basic learning and enrichment that are inherent in the film technique, and the classrooms in which they teach do little to encourage them. Although

15. *The Principals Look at the Schools,* pp. 23-24. Working paper prepared for the Project on Instruction. Washington: National Education Association, 1962.

film and television today form an integral part of a student's life outside the school, they still constitute a rarity in the classroom.

The duplication of high-school studies in the freshman year of college has long been a problem in American education, a problem which has been accentuated by the recent pre-collegiate curriculum reform. A program that has come to be known as Advanced Placement, paralleling the current curriculum reform, is easing the problem for several thousand able students each year, but its potential and that of related procedures to provide acceleration and continuity in learning have scarcely been tapped.

Supported by a grant from the Fund for the Advancement of Education, representatives of twelve colleges and twelve high schools in 1952 organized the School and College Study of Admission with Advanced Standing (also known as the Kenyon Plan because it originated during a faculty discussion at Kenyon College). The group proposed that students, instead of moving out of high school, remain there but do college work in one or more subjects, qualifying them for admission to college with advanced standing or placement in their chosen field.

Seven schools cooperated in the experiment, allowing their able students to take special courses designed by the study group and examinations prepared by an outside agency. The purpose of the study was to answer two questions: 1) Could basic freshmen courses be sufficiently defined to convince college and university faculties that the prescribed work done in secondary school was the equivalent of work done in college, and 2) are bright high-school students able to do college-level work?

The first examinations were produced in 1954, and a year later the College Entrance Examination Board assumed financial and administrative responsibility for the program, thus giving it national status. The program now operates through a director, an Advanced Placement (AP) Committee, and eleven subject-matter committees. It offers high-school students college-level work in American and European history, English, French, German, Latin, Spanish, biology, chemistry, physics, and mathematics.

Students usually prepare themselves for advanced standing or credit by taking an AP course in the 11th or 12th grade. These courses, intended for the better-than-average and superior student, follow a specified outline and culminate in an examination. Grades are sent to the institution the student is entering and the decision to grant credit, or advanced placement, or both, is left to that institution.

The remarkable growth of the program is indicated by the fact that in 1966 examinations were administered to about 38,000 candidates from 2,500 high schools as compared with the initial group of 1,229 students from 104 schools. And yet, despite its proved value, the program is reaching only a small number of schools—some 2,500 out of a possible 18,000. Growing interest, however, in the individualization of instruction and the continuous improvement of school organization suggest that the Advanced Placement approach is likely to increase in attractiveness. Some estimates predict that by 1971 the number of participating secondary schools will have grown to 3,600.

Also compatible with individualized instruction and improved school organization are those plans that reorganize schools vertically into multi-graded or non-graded programs, and horizontally into various cooperative teaching arrangements. The non-graded scheme is compatible with a curriculum planned around themes, principles, concepts, and modes of inquiry that are being developed over many years of schooling, replacing a curriculum that consists of bits and pieces, and daily or weekly time blocks of instruction. Team teaching developed, in part, because it was felt that students need teachers who possess a thorough knowledge of their subject field as well as a real understanding of the school's function.

Greater awareness of the fact that a large number of students do not seem to profit from the fare the schools offer has resulted in a plethora of proposals to educate the slow learners, the academically talented, and the physically handicapped. And the realization that automation is bringing about employment problems of a kind that has never been experienced before has helped to revitalize the field of vocational and technical education.

At the lower end of the educational scale, hundreds of thousands of four- and five-year-olds from culturally deprived environments are being helped by Project Head Start to begin school less intellectually handicapped than otherwise would be the case. The effectiveness of this early education program is just beginning to be evaluated. Head Start may well be the prelude to a general downward extension of public education, if recent recommendations of the NEA's Educational Policies Commission for four-year-olds' schooling come to fruition.

The curricular contributions of the supplementary, regional, and research and development laboratories (now being established under Titles III and IV of the Elementary and Secondary Education Act of 1965) cannot yet be estimated. But never before have educators enjoyed such financial largesse for activities that are designed to accomplish more than to maintain a minimum educational floor.

In all this turmoil—some of it denoting progress, some of it not—a faint glimmer of light is growing stronger: the belief that, increasingly, curriculum reforms will be based on the cultivation of the individual and the assurance of a self-renewing society, whereas the curriculum revisions of the past were largely a result of pressures for the preservation of society.

PROBLEMS
AND ISSUES

There is more to planning an effective curriculum in English, geography or biology than merely arranging topics in an ascending order of difficulty believed to be inherent in the subject. As a matter of fact, what finally appears as the students' learning fare should be the end product of a series of decisions made deliberately and consciously rather than by default. The nature of these decisions is itself a significant realm of inquiry, and one that has been little explored. Nevertheless, some work has been done in this area, and curriculum planners would do well to examine the existing literature before they become involved in the problems and issues of planning.

A substantial number of the new crop of reformers have approached the persistent, recurring problems of curriculum development in the naive belief that no one had ever looked at them before. This may be "discovery," but it is not disciplined discovery; the wise explorer studies the maps of those who went before. Nor is it an economical use of time and money. But there are now some signs that a modern curriculum dialogue is developing and that it might even be joined with the productive dialogue of yesterday.[16]

Stripped to the bone, curriculum dialogue takes as its subject matter the ends and means of education and schooling: What shall be the overall aims of education? What objectives shall the schools take for themselves? What is worth knowing? How shall the curriculum be organized?

Has the current curriculum reform movement addressed itself to these questions and, if so, in what way?

---

16. See, for example, Lawrence A. Cremin, *The Genius of American Education* (particularly pp. 37-63). Pittsburgh: University of Pittsburgh Press, 1965.

Aims and Objectives

There is a striking similarity in the aims and objectives of the projects described in Section II. The term "aims" as used here refers to the more general and remote ends of schooling. The term "objectives" refers to the purposes as they apply to students.

Objectives stress the importance of understanding the structure of the discipline, the purposes and methods of the field, and the part that creative men and women have played in developing the field. A major objective of nearly all projects is to afford students an opportunity to explore, invent, and discover; to develop some of the tools of inquiry appropriate to the field; and to experience some of the feelings and satisfactions of research scholars. A more distant aim is to prepare the student for intellectual and academic survival in a complex, scientific world. Such traditional social aims as preparation for citizenship or for intelligent participation in decisions facing the community are only rarely mentioned. In fact, even the objectives of subject fields are seldom made explicit and usually must be inferred.

Little effort has been made to determine the ultimate aims of schooling and the respective contribution each discipline can make to them. Instead, the objectives of schooling have become a composite of the objectives set for each subject. These objectives, in turn, seem to rest on the assumption that any significant concept or mode of behavior that can be derived from analysis of an academic discipline can be learned by students of a given age and is thus worth learning. It can be expected, therefore, that subjects constituting the present curriculum will be examined first to determine what students should seek to attain. And this is precisely what has happened. The goals of today's schools do not extend beyond those subjects that have succeeded in establishing themselves in the curriculum.

Persons involved in the various curriculum projects are not and, indeed, should not be solely responsible for determining the aims of America's schools. This responsibility falls to the citizenry as a whole. The fact that our communities, generally speaking, have not assumed this responsibility has resulted in a vacuum against which the validity of the projects' objectives cannot be checked. The objectives of the several subject-field projects have become, therefore—by default as it were—the educational aims of the communities adopting the various project courses.

"How does a community decide which value patterns are to be taught in its schools and are to be used as a basis for curricular and instructional decisions? . . . One possible answer is that a pluralistic society wishes for an obvious and open decision never to occur. A struggle of this sort would be divisive, indicating quite clearly to a number of subgroups that their views were not being adopted by the society as a whole. Thus a pluralistic society may prefer to ignore this question as long as possible in the hope that it will not become too troublesome. Some aspects of our present educational situation suggest that in part we have more or less consciously adopted this answer."[17]

To determine what students ought to learn on the basis of what is significant to a discipline and what can be learned by a majority of the students causes some difficulty. The concepts of energy, number, and evolution, which are significant to physics, mathematics, and biology, can be learned in an academically acceptable way by young children. (The optimum time for learning them, however, still remains to be empirically determined.) But suppose we find that a range of concepts, running the gamut of twenty or more disciplines, can be learned by young children? Since limitations in time necessitate choice, what criteria do we use to guide our choices? Clearly, some more fundamental validation than the ability of children to learn certain concepts is needed to help us choose among a number of alternatives. The problem is no less pressing at the high-school level where, in order to set up a social studies curriculum, for example, criteria other than student capability are required to arrive at an intelligent choice among history, geography, economics, political science, sociology, and anthropology.

One long-term solution is for state and local boards of education to agree on the purposes and objectives of our schools. This they have not done or seem about to do.

A short-term answer is for project committees to justify goals beyond the parochial limits of disciplines and children's abilities to learn them.

17. Harold B. Dunkel, "Value Decisions and the Public Schools," *School Review,* 70 (Summer, 1962), p. 165.

And some projects are moving in just that direction. Project directors have become increasingly sensitive to the human processes that appear to transcend the methods presumed to be unique to the discipline. "Science—A Process Approach," for example, seeks cultivation of such methods as observation, classification, communication, inference, and prediction. These are not unique to science but are equally appropriate to the enjoyment of literature and artistic performance—and to the full development of man's rational powers.

The lack of stated aims for education has virtually forced curriculum project groups to turn to school subjects for the determination of their ends and means. As a consequence, ends and means frequently become hopelessly entwined: to learn the subject is the end; learning the subject is the means. There is no external criterion against which to judge the effectiveness of the new or the old. Because the new purports to do something different, it is presumed to be better. But, given this presumption, the next step is to prove the new is superior by demonstrating that it does this "something different" better. What is needed are evaluative criteria in the form of educational objectives that have been agreed on, quite apart from the specific claims to virtue made by this or that approach to curriculum organization.

Curriculum planners, in general, have been delinquent in stating their educational objectives with precision. Few statements satisfy the criteria for objectives set forth by Mager:

"1) An instructional objective describes an intended outcome rather than a description or summary of content. 2) One characteristic of a usefully stated objective is that it is stated in behavioral, or performance, terms that describe what the learner will be *doing* when demonstrating his achievement of the objective. 3) The statement of objectives for an entire program of instruction will consist of several specific statements. 4) The objective . . . most usefully stated is one which best communicates the instructional intent of the person selecting the objective."[18]

What are intended to be objectives more often than not turn out to be general statements of intent, propositions about learning rather than achievements expected of learners, or even descriptions of courses. Ad-

18. Robert F. Mager, *Preparing Objectives for Programmed Instruction,* p. 24. San Francisco: Fearon Publishers, 1962.

mittedly, the intuitive grasp or glimpse of an abstract objective sought by many subject-matter projects is not easily defined. But how can teachers teach for it or evaluate it unless they know what this intuition consists of? What is the terminal behavior expected of the student? What does he do when he has acquired it? Let us not answer these questions the way Louis Armstrong responded to the query, what is jazz?: "If I have to explain it, you'll never understand."

Organization

The various projects almost uniformly seek to present tightly organized courses in which important ideas appear and reappear, with cumulative detail designed to develop these ideas in increasing depth. It is in the organization of courses that the basic difference between "the old" and "the new" arrangements becomes apparent. In the old arrangement, topic followed topic; there were few attempts to reveal what lay behind their order. The new arrangement still presents many topics, but interspersed among them are reminders, for example, of the importance of careful observation, or of the relationship between a given topic and a concept that the topic is designed to illuminate.

At least three techniques are used to effect these interrelationships. The first, well represented by the Physical Science Study Committee's course, is a single, unified sequence employing many different media—textbooks, laboratory experiments, films, and books on special topics—with each medium playing its particular role. But no one of these, neither the textbook, nor the laboratory experiment, nor the film, is a substitute for anything else; each plays its part as in an orchestra, and each contributes to the final results. The second technique is partially illustrated by the Chemical Bond Approach course, where text and program are designed to run side by side as well as to reinforce each other; each part works independently of the other and is capable, at least to a degree, of standing alone. Admittedly, this high-school chemistry course would be weakened by the omission of one of them, since each part alone has a certain integrity. The third technique, illustrated in some of the materials produced by the AAAS's Commission of Science Education, identifies the major elements of the course, programs each of these side by side, and makes a deliberate effort to relate them at strategic points.

These three approaches are essentially methods of curriculum organization. To some degree, they reflect differing views of how learning can best be effected. Parallel laboratory and textbook study suggests that the concepts of a course can be learned through experimentation as well as from a textbook. Laboratory activity alternating with textbook study suggests that some things are learned best through experimentation while others may be learned through reading and discussion. Most of the courses reflect the assumption that each medium has its appropriate use, with its strengths and weaknesses depending on the immediate instructional purpose.

The course of the Chemical Education Material Study, reflecting the first approach, serves to illustrate the interweaving of methods or concepts and of specific topics designed to develop these scientific concepts and methods. An initial statement of justification for the course sets the tone: "The citizen must have an improved awareness of the significance and capabilities of scientific activities because of the impact of the resulting technological advances on his social environment." This view is developed in the course by defining the basic activities of science as follows: "to accumulate information through observation; to organize this information and to seek regularities in it; to wonder why the regularities exist; to communicate the findings to others." Project statements frequently refer to the "capabilities of scientific *activities*" and to the "basic activities of *science.*" The non-scientist would have used, more likely "men" instead of "activities" and "scientists" instead of "science." Clearly, science is the beginning and the end of the new curricula in science.

The first test of a scheme of curricular organization lies in the relationship between the organizing center (topic, problem, question) used to involve the student, and the central concepts (element, compound, model) and methods (observation, generalization, communication) that the student is to learn. Too much of the first in relation to the second, and the course reverts to what it is designed to replace—a coverage of facts, facts, facts. Too much of the second in relation to the first, and the course becomes a kind of preaching about the nature and virtues of science and what scientists do. The student needs a moderate number of carefully chosen facts to chew on. But the nutritive element lies within, like the vitamins in natural food.

The second test determines what the student has really digested. Has the nutritive element become part of him or does he merely converse glibly about what he appears to have consumed? Although there is a vast difference between these possibilities, the task of distinguishing between them is very complex.

Curriculum projects designed to prepare course materials in separate subjects avoid many of the most crucial problems of scope and sequence in the program of a school. For some years at least, the pattern in mathematics and the natural sciences at the high-school level appears to be set: physics, biology, and chemistry are established as separate courses that exist side by side or alternate in successive years. Eventually some study group will examine the fact that atomic and molecular models, for example, are not the exclusive property of a single science, and will describe how they are treated in the several courses. Such analyses are necessary prerequisites to future efforts to synthesize several divisions of science. Unpopular as such an idea may be today, synthetic approaches are likely to be on the ascendency after the current movement has resulted in widespread reform. Change is characteristic of the human race and change, by definition, is a moving away from what exists. Before long reforming educators, no doubt, will speak once again of a segmented curriculum and the need for general studies to remedy that situation.

The relevance of this discussion is not missed by the workers in the elementary-school curriculum vineyard, many of whom are acutely aware of the problems and issues involved in choosing among the divisions of knowledge, to say nothing of the subjects within each division. Robert Karplus (Science Curriculum Improvement Study), for example, is making a significant attempt to incorporate concepts from the biological sciences into what started out as a project heavily slanted toward the physical sciences. Such efforts at the lower levels of schooling may ultimately influence planning at the higher levels—the reverse of what has commonly occurred in the past.

The emerging patterns in the social sciences and humanities at the high-school level, and in most fields at the elementary-school level, are not at all clear, although the separate-subject doctrine dominates. There is some prospect of alternating the social sciences in the high school, with history, for example, dominating for perhaps a semester, and other fields being subordinated. Some of the more interesting possibilities of rotating students in the various arts, so that they will receive a broad exposure in both appreciation and performance, depend in part upon what will emerge from elementary-school programs. But curriculum revision at that level has so far been peripheral or, as in the field of mathematics, has consisted merely of a downward extension of steps closely geared to those already established for the secondary school.

As curriculum planning extends downward, reformers increasingly are struck by the fact that a good deal of material encased in the subject sheath at the high-school level has no logical downward extension. What are the roots of physics and chemistry, for example, other than those already introduced in the new courses for grades 10 or 11? The current curriculum reform movement has reconditioned shockingly outworn courses and has given us a fresh way of approaching various subject fields—a fresh way as regards school practice, if not curriculum theory. But planning from the top down has in some instances brought with it a straitjacket, incongruously ill-suited to childhood schooling. A really significant reform movement, therefore, looks ahead to a time when the curriculum will be planned from the bottom up, with knowledge of students and their achievements built into the sequence of subject matter in the curriculum design. Such a movement will be marked by experimentation and by the emergence of alternatives greatly exceeding the number that have evolved so far from the current curriculum projects.

Evaluation

To date, at least four different means of evaluating new programs have been used: 1) observations of whether or not the students for whom the material is intended appear to be progressing successfully; 2) both casual and systematic questioning of students involved in the programs; 3) periodic examination of students by tests designed to cover the new material; and 4) comparative testing of students in the new and the old programs with traditional and specially designed tests.

In the early years of the projects, the cooperating schools usually were those with teachers and students of superior ability. Furthermore, the teachers participated in special institutes and had access to counsel of various kinds. Even in later years, the participating schools tended not to be in depressed areas; the students rarely were in the bottom quartile of the ability distribution but often were in the top half; and almost all the teachers, because of the close liaison with project headquarters, considered themselves "part of the enterprise." It is not surprising, therefore, to learn that project staffs have received highly satisfactory reactions from students and teachers.

The testimonials would fill several volumes. Students have commented particularly on the satisfaction they derive from the opportunity to work independently, often on problems of their own choosing. Some have spoken of their disappointment with "cut-and-dried" college courses after their adventures with one or more of the new high-school courses. Teachers have at times become eloquent over finding a new challenge in teaching. Certainly, many of the new courses—with their more interesting and carefully programed textbooks, laboratory manuals, teachers' guides, and films—have given teachers help of a kind they have rarely enjoyed before. While this enthusiasm must be viewed with some caution, the fact that many of the textbooks have appeared and reappeared in trial editions, thus remaining somewhat experimental in character, adds to the validity of these comments. Actually, negative comments refer most frequently to aspects of trial and error: explanations were not sufficiently clear, complexity of the material increased too quickly, individual differences had not been sufficiently considered, and so on. But in general, the participating students and teachers have felt that the curricula of the American high school and, to a lesser degree, of the elementary school have received a shot in the arm.

Most new courses are designed with content and emphases different from those of the usual high-school courses. Therefore, special tests are needed. "One does not often try to determine electrical current with a meter stick or lengths with an ammeter; we must be equally careful in trying to measure the successes of courses that differ in kind, rather than degree, by using a test intended for one as instrument to calibrate the other."[19]

Some special tests have been prepared and used both to determine the success of students in achieving the objectives of the new courses and—together with traditional tests—to compare students in old and new programs. The testing programs of the Physical Science Study Committee and of the Biological Sciences Curriculum Study are representative examples of internal evaluation and of attempts to determine whether course objectives are being met. Both projects included relatively long-term testing in their plans almost from the beginning.

The results of comparing students in new and old programs on the basis of new and old tests are quite similar from field to field. Students in conventional programs do relatively well on conventional tests; however, on tests prepared for the revised courses they do poorly in comparison with students in the new programs. In addition, students in new courses often do as well as students in conventional courses when the traditional tests call for problem-solving abilities and do not require the recall of specific terms or facts.

Some of the internal evaluations have brought forth interesting information on the comparative success of students of varying abilities and varying past performances. A surprisingly high percentage of low-ability students have outperformed many of their very able fellow students. Similarly, students with mediocre past performances in a certain subject have surprised themselves and their teachers in a revised version of that subject. The data suggest that at least some students are finding what is essentially a fresh start. In a school system organized to provide few second chances, this in itself is a meaningful change.

A significant kind of internal evaluation, characteristic of several projects, involves the assessment of the sequencing or programing of learning stimuli. Ideally, each step is programed so that a truly hierarchical structure of learning sets is produced. Each set is a logical and slightly more advanced progression from the previous one. Failure of a student to perform the final task indicates either that he did not complete the sequence as instructed or that the gaps from set to set are of such

19. Francis L. Friedman and associates, "The Relation of the PSSC Physics Course to Conventional High School Courses," *Science Teacher,* 29 (February, 1962), pp. 49-55.

magnitude that the student was derailed. In computer-based instruction, the student's progress is monitored as he progresses and his or the program's deficiencies are detected immediately. Diagnosis of the problem presumably leads to a new prescription for the student, for the program, or for both.[20]

A fundamental assumption is that good programing enables students of relatively low ability and poor past performance to progress satisfactorily when otherwise they would have failed or accumulated debilitating learning deficiencies. The viability of this assumption is borne out, in part at least, by the number of students who have far surpassed their previous performances in the same but not yet revised subjects. We have here a theory of curriculum planning that, if supported by experimental research, would have tremendous implications, particularly for general education. Everything within man's knowledge becomes available to all students, once it is programed effectively.

But the time factor looms threateningly. What happens to the student who requires a large amount of time for a small portion of accomplishment? Is the proportion of learning accomplished, albeit successfully, so minor in relation to the learning to be accomplished that profound discouragement sets in? What if his limited ability carries him successfully through 7th-grade mathematics but his energies flag in the 8th grade? Or will each individual triumph so motivate him that he will tackle the next task with renewed vigor?

A second aspect of time leads us to the question of value, as regards both the individual and society. If a relatively slow student can acquire the subject matter—assuming that it is programed carefully, he is given enough time, and that what he learns contributes significantly to his personal development and the welfare of society—then the added costs of making it available to him are probably justified. The amount of time actually allowed the student—a factor that determines his success and most likely his continuation in the subject and in school—will vary with the affluence of the society and its willingness to support education for all. Yet the appropriateness of fields of learning must not be determined

20. John I. Goodlad, "Diagnosis and Prescription in Educational Practice," *New Approaches to Individualizing Instruction*, pp. 27-37. Princeton, N. J.: Educational Testing Service, 1965.

only by the student's ability to comprehend. At some point we must inquire whether a specific field has relevance for a specific student in relation to the other fields making a demand on his time. Further, we must inquire at what stages of his development certain areas of knowledge are most easily acquired and when, therefore, his time and society's resources can be used most economically. Such inquiries are markedly absent from today's curriculum reform movement.

Instruction

The end product of curriculum planning is a challenge to the learner: a problem, question, statement, or description to which students or groups of students are expected to respond. As mentioned previously, many problems and issues must be resolved in the process of producing effective learning opportunities or stimuli. Another cluster of issues, not inherent in curriculum development per se but of crucial significance, pertains to the role of the teacher. Are the new materials intended to be transmitted to the students through the teacher or directly? If the former, are new skills or attitudes required? If the latter, is the teacher to have merely a supervisory role?

The dominant position in current curriculum reform is that the teacher is of prime importance. In the early years of the movement, project staffs considered in-service teacher education to be almost as important as curriculum revision itself. Accordingly, they provided summer and all-year institutes, answering services to deal with teachers' questions, short-term conferences, and other kinds of teacher help. Some groups required in-service teacher education as a condition for gaining access to the materials.

In projects making extensive use of programing, however, there has been relatively little commitment to changing the teacher's role beyond gaining his willingness to introduce the materials into the classroom. Superb programing presumably renders materials "teacher-proof." But even if programed instruction will ultimately reach this point in all fields, a teacherless educational enterprise appears to be a most unlikely eventuality. The teacher remains a meaningful element in any curriculum reform.

During recent years in-service teacher education has played a less important role in some curriculum projects. As paperback editions of project textbooks move into hard-cover versions and as commercial publishers incorporate new concepts and organizational patterns into their wares, teachers' manuals appear to be increasingly designed to eliminate the need for special teacher education.

The writer's own observations in many of the classrooms that are using the newer curriculum materials—many of these classrooms participated as trial centers—confirm the importance of preparing teachers in the underlying assumptions and concepts of the new materials. Many teachers simply cannot adapt themselves to what is required. Long conditioned to deductive approaches, they turn materials intended for student investigation into objects of rote response.

Traditionally, teaching has been a telling procedure. In general, students have not been encouraged to explore, invent, discover, and create. Stress on inductive processes in the ends and means of the newer curricular enterprises introduces into the classroom an essentially foreign element. Teachers are being asked to preside over a fundamentally different kind of learning-teaching process. To think that they will make the transformation easily is naive.

Teacher orientation to the intent, procedures, and products of some curriculum projects has been minimal, and has sometimes been confined to a week-long workshop or less. Teachers usually are introduced to the mechanics but not to the concepts and principles. Those whose teaching repertoires include proficiency in inductive procedures thrive; the others continue in their long-established ways.

Clearly, curriculum planners must not stop with the production of materials. If the proposed changes are worth introducing at all, then they must be introduced thoroughly with careful attention to every component of the change process. The intent of the new curricula is not adequately comprehended by large numbers of teachers now using them. And neither the general nor the professional curriculum of prospective teachers reflects the point of view of the curricula for which they soon will be responsible.

The answers to the central questions of curriculum planning are probably no more obscure today than they have been at other times. The problem seems always to be that of developing an awareness of the essential curriculum questions to be answered. Also, curriculum planning is always circumscribed by the realities of the larger social context within which it occurs. The concluding section of this report examines the current movement in relation to this larger context.

CONCLUSION

Balance in the Curriculum

The problem of maintaining balance in the curriculum is a constant challenge to educators. The factors producing an imbalance lie in three major areas:

First, program development in the social sciences, humanities (especially the arts), health, and physical education is still in the beginning stages at both elementary and secondary levels of education. There is some activity in all of these fields but it does not compare in intensity or accomplishment with what has already transpired in mathematics, physics, chemistry, and biology.

Although the National Science Foundation has demonstrated some broadening of interests, projects in the physical and biological sciences have so far received priority. But now, largely as a result of recently enacted legislation, the Office of Education is in a position to correct the imbalance through greater stress on the social sciences and humanities. The Social Studies Program, the English Program, and the establishment of the Arts and Humanities Program are promising developments.

The second aspect of imbalance lies in the fact that many subjects that could be part of the curriculum are not included. Many social sciences, for example, are left out or included only peripherally. Are they to remain outside the fold, to be brought in as separate subjects, or are they to be combined with other subjects in what is sometimes referred to as a broad-field curriculum? There has been little effort to combine related fields; in fact, the current movement is predicated upon the discreteness of subjects and the importance of organizing and teaching them as separate disciplines. How are the social sciences to be arranged? If anthropology, sociology, economics, political science, and psychology are to have a place in the pre-collegiate curriculum, are they to stand alone or are they to be joined with history and geography in a synthesized social studies program?

In view of the fact that not all fields can ever be included in the curriculum, efforts must be made to combine the concepts of those fields that have been left out with the concepts of those already included. The combining of several social sciences into a social studies curriculum provides areas for fruitful exploration; the possibilities for organizing curricula in the humanities around unifying elements that have been selected from several subjects also present a considerable challenge. Project staffs, furthermore, might tackle the problem of alternating graphic and plastic arts, music, dance, and drama while seeking to develop elementary or secondary-school curricula in the arts. If this country is to move beyond its present adolescence in the performing arts, they will have to become a part of the regular schooling of all children and youth.

The third consideration of imbalance is the piecemeal school curriculum produced by adopting several programs that have been prepared independently of each other. It is left largely to the schools to choose between the "old" and the "new," to select from among several varieties of the new in some fields (mathematics, for example), to determine time allocations, to establish patterns of continuity from elementary to secondary schools, and so on. These difficulties are compounded for local schools by student transiency and the fact that, in many parts of the country, elementary and secondary-school districts are separately organized and administered. Such problems are not likely to be solved within the patterns of the current curriculum reform movement as they now exist.

What is needed are experimental efforts designed to create models of pre-collegiate curricula, extending from kindergarten through grade

.12 and including all standard subjects or combinations of subjects. Such models would serve to demonstrate how programs in the new mathematics, physics, chemistry, biology, and other fields might be fitted together, and to point up the resultant problems of time utilization, continuity, and balance. Two kinds of projects might be useful: those seeking to establish experimental schools in which comprehensive curricula could be demonstrated, and those seeking to simulate the curricula of feasible but nonexistent schools.

The first type of project probably can be conducted best by local school districts (with supplementary federal or state support) that are willing to designate pilot schools and avail themselves of competent help from neighboring universities. One such venture is the League of Cooperating Schools, consisting of some twenty schools from a like number of independent school districts in southern California, which is supported by the University of California, Los Angeles, and the Institute for Development of Educational Activities.

The second type of project fits best into curriculum study centers located in universities with access to the data and problems of neighboring schools. Using computer-based techniques, such centers would be able to simulate curricula for all elementary and secondary education. Specific curriculum products could be analyzed and problems anticipated before school districts actually encounter them. The University of Minnesota has already created the nucleus of such a study center.

Before long it will also be necessary to identify and chart the differences and similarities of the concepts and behaviors inherent in the different curriculum designs of one discipline. Such an analysis would go a long way toward ensuring curricular sequence and correlation and preventing mere duplication. It would also help in planning a reasonable allocation of time, which is always in short supply.

The department of education in each state should be well informed about school and university curricular activities so it can assist school districts likely to be faced with problems. Through such involvement, state education departments might play a more meaningful role in curriculum development than they have done so far; efforts to clarify their proper function in this area and to formulate guidelines for local school districts are long overdue.

Experimentation

The current curriculum reform movement has been experimental in only a limited sense. Certain assumptions, goals, and ways of achieving these goals have been set forth in advance: students are to understand basic principles on a more than merely informational level of cognition, to develop modes of inquiry inherent in the field, and to appreciate and identify with the work of the scholar. This is to be achieved through text and class activities organized around fundamental concepts, through laboratory experimentation, and through films or other devices portraying the scholar's investigations. Experimentation under these circumstances becomes largely a process of refinement through which the means are polished until they satisfy the critical appraisal of teacher and student alike. Rarely, if at all, are two or more sets of means contrasted with each other and compared as to their effectiveness in achieving a given objective.

However, the great number of different projects in the various subject fields does supply us with some alternatives; for a while, at least, we have the "old" and the "new." But the difficulty in comparing the old with the new curriculum, as stated in the previous section, is the general lack of precise educational objectives and measuring tools common to and appropriate for both. Several projects are beginning to develop sensitive tests to evaluate their own objectives, but there remains the problem of identifying generally acceptable evaluative criteria.

It is important to create alternative patterns within the new curriculum lest it become a monolithic movement. Two or more investigators, committed to the same ends and comparable evaluative techniques, should experiment with different means to meet these ends. This type of experiment, virtually nonexistent until now, will have to be conducted on a large scale if we want to have the kind of curriculum science that enables us to predict, with some precision, the chances of achieving a given end with a given means.

Investigators might well devote special attention to experiments using basically different approaches to attain a fixed set of educational objectives. Encouragement should be given to projects designed to do the following: 1) develop curricular sequences from the bottom up instead of from the top down, thus opening up interesting possibilities for relating longitudinal subject-matter sequences to the developmental processes of children and youth; 2) compare patterns organized around single subjects with patterns combining or alternating several related subjects; 3) develop and test materials with children and youth representing divergent cultural groups, especially from disadvantaged environments; 4) study the advantages and disadvantages of the various learning styles represented in large groups of students; 5) experiment with materials and techniques that challenge and hold the interests of students with widely varying motives, abilities, and past educational attainments.

Although project staffs have tried their materials in many instances with a variety of population groups, there has been very little true experimentation in the sense of comparing alternatives. In the early years, materials were developed and refined almost entirely with suburban schools and school districts—the higher socioeconomic, college-bound populations. Subsequently, project staffs have trial-taught the same materials with more generally representative populations and have been gratified to find that their products stood up reasonably well. But this process of refinement is different from that of developing alternatives for comparative testing with a variety of populations. There are indications that such experimental approaches are being planned but at present they are still in short supply.

A curriculum predicated on research and experimentation ultimately changes the relationship between project offices and schools. Project staffs will no longer be just the purveyors of a new "instructional package," but will now want some of the student's time to test their notions on him. In return they will offer a contribution to knowledge, a comprehensive report, and improved curriculum materials. Most school officials seek to cooperate with the projects but there are limits. Few boards are likely to approve the release of students from approved curricula for the long periods of time that are required to develop and test truly experimental alternatives.

Laboratory schools maintained by universities (or by school systems and universities collaboratively) for purposes of research, experimentation, and inquiry in education are generally less restricted. Unfortunately, few of these institutions have taken advantage of their freedom. In fact, most appear to be committed not to advancing the theory and practice of education but to maintaining the status quo. What we sorely need is a rejuvenation of the experimental quest, and particularly in those schools that are part of the research environment in major universities.

Self-Renewal

Broad-scale implementation of current curriculum projects depends upon both the usefulness of materials produced and the in-service edution of the teachers who use them. Most projects have distinguished themselves on both accounts. Continuing self-renewal of the current curriculum reform movement, however, depends upon the pre-service preparation of teachers in the new content and its accompanying pedagogy, and the education of teachers who understand and are sympathetic to the role organized subject matter plays in the education of the young. Unfortunately, current projects have not distinguished themselves on this account.

Future teachers who will have studied the reformed pre-collegiate and collegiate curricula will presumably possess the content they need for up-to-date teaching. But a supply of such teachers is some years in the offing. We must furthermore assume that insights into the nature of knowledge and into how knowledge should be organized and taught for most effective learning will change. Most likely we will gain more insight into such matters during the next decade than we have acquired during the past half century. We must realize then that today's teachers are not well equipped to teach tomorrow's pre-collegiate curricula. It is imperative, therefore, to find ways and means to familiarize these teachers, regardless of their past training, with current content, methods, and techniques.

Prospective teachers also will have to be trained in the processes and concepts that they in turn have to develop in their students. Teachers and teachers of teachers alike must get their hands dirty and their minds involved in the "stuff" of learning. In other words, if teachers are to promote the inductive reasoning of the young, they must experience such reasoning themselves, or they subvert the inquiry intended, no matter how good the materials prepared for their use. Perhaps, some teachers' courses could be taught by "clinical professors"[21]—top-level personnel teaching the new content in neighboring schools—with the approval of the university's education department and appropriate other departments. The possibilities for cooperation between schools and universities, and in addition among departments within universities, are indeed challenging.

Adequate arrangements to educate a continuous stream of teachers in what and how they are to teach depend upon a kind of cooperation between the department of education and other departments that has as yet developed on only a few campuses. Mutual respect and understanding have been lacking and are not likely to emerge from debate and casual discussion. Desirable conditions for productive work cannot be established until both groups have agreed on a problem of mutual interest and on their respective contributions to it. To educate new teachers in the content and pedagogy of their disciplines and in the curricular problems of teaching and educating the young constitutes such a problem—one which the curriculum reform movement is at present neglecting.

The responsibility of preparing teachers of teachers and students of education rests with the department or school of education. This is a fact of academic life that is not likely to change even in the distant future, and a fact that is being overlooked in the present processes of curriculum change. The trainers of teachers are not learning enough about the new curriculum movement; and the students of education are not including it in their investigations. While the current curriculum reform is closing a long-standing gap between curricular theory and school practice, it has not been able so far to influence the content and pedagogy in those colleges and universities that prepare tomorrow's teachers, educational leaders, and teachers of teachers. And until it does, it has no means for self-renewal.

---

21. For a discussion of the clinical professor concept in the education of teachers, see James B. Conant, *The Education of American Teachers,* pp. 140-145. New York: McGraw-Hill, 1963.

Authority and Responsibility

The interest of the federal government in supporting curriculum development, first through the National Science Foundation and more recently through the Office of Education, has raised some important issues regarding authority and responsibility. There is no question that federal influence on what children and youth learn in school has increased during recent years.

But the fear of a "national curriculum" appears unwarranted. The balance among subjects has been affected, but there has been no movement toward a standard learning fare for all. In fact, there has been a gratifying array of different projects in most of the fields that receive federal funds, and the curriculum today is considerably more varied than when it was determined almost entirely by textbook publishers, their writers, and consultants.

The entry into the "education industry" of business giants such as the Radio Corporation of America, Columbia Broadcasting System, General Electric and others, promises competition in the production of materials, and a nearly unlimited number of instructional alternatives. More than that, it suggests a changing role for the federal government, which, instead of being concerned with the immediate impact of the curriculum, can now attend to matters of national direction, including an appropriate distribution of educational responsibilities among our major governing bodies.

Two other issues raised by the federal involvement in curriculum reform are worth mentioning. The first pertains to the complex publishing arrangements relating to the production and distribution of project materials. In most instances, commercial publishers are free to pick up and use the new curriculum ideas as they emanate from project activities, with the provision only that appropriate credit be given. There are instances, however, where a project director signs a contract awarding one commercial house exclusive rights for production and distribution. Such a contract usually provides for the royalties to be used in support of further research and development. Nevertheless, the publisher reaps certain rewards that in part are the result of a federal investment.

This interplay of public and private funds and agencies for common welfare is not new to American life, but it warrants greater attention and closer scrutiny.

The second issue relates to the apparent lack of curriculum planning at state and local educational levels. The task is simply too great to be assumed by local districts. The instructional packages prepared by the SMSG, the PSSC, the SCIS and the other projects are infinitely superior to those turned out by all but a handful of very large school systems. The ease with which the project materials are utilized by the local schools reveals furthermore what some analysts of public policy have known for a long time: that boards of education are neglecting part of their responsibility by not determining the basic policies and goals for their schools. In fact, most boards are not certain what their authority and responsibilities are.

The situation is not much different at the state level where decisions made at the local level are often duplicated and others, relevant to the states, are neglected. Curriculum directives tend more often than not to be a hodgepodge, resulting from frequently ill-coordinated, onetime decisions of the state legislatures.

The federal government is providing direct assistance to state departments of education through Title V of the Elementary and Secondary Education Act of 1965. Some of the funds are being used for critical self-analyses and other studies of an analytical nature that are long overdue. Growing out of the Compact for Education, the Education Commission of the States in 1966 established itself as an official national congress of educational methods, policies, and directives of the states.[22] Whether or not the commission will serve as a buffer between the states and the federal government in educational matters or as a means to shape educational policy in the individual states is a question that cannot be answered as yet.

We have spoken of the need for curriculum study centers. It would be most desirable if at least one of them would study the respective responsibilities of local, state, and federal educational offices, and how each of these is or is not assuming its responsibilities.

---

22. See *The Compact for Education*. Durham, North Carolina: Duke University, 1965.

Tomorrow

Thanks to the willingness of scholars to concern themselves with pre-collegiate education (something they were patently reluctant to do until recently), to the interest of a few psychologists in pedagogical problems, and to the enthusiasm of the teachers who were brought into the curriculum reform, the curricula in most fields have been or are being rejuvenated. The structure of academic disciplines stands at the center of curriculum planning and characterizes the very objectives, organizational patterns, and subject matter. The work of the past fifteen years, including the identification of the concepts, principles, and methods of inquiry worth teaching and learning, has provided a dimension to the undertaking that tomorrow's curriculum reformers cannot ignore.

But subject matter is not the whole of curriculum, any more than a jet airplane is the whole of transportation. Not all subjects can be included in a school's curriculum. Not everything a child can learn is necessarily something he should learn. Questions pertaining to a balanced curriculum are not likely to be answered through individual projects in separate disciplines, nor should the answers be left to subject specialists alone. Questions regarding the total curriculum—at all levels of education—belong on tomorrow's educational agenda. But perhaps a different choice of procedures and of groupings of people will be necessary if they are to be dealt with wisely and well.

One other important question remains which has scarcely been asked at all: What kinds of persons do we wish our schools to produce? We suggest that it be made the focal point of tomorrow's curriculum deliberations and of many more discussions to come.

SELECTED READINGS

Below is a brief, annotated list of readings divided into three groups. The first is a sample of pamphlets, reports, collections of articles, and books that describe or otherwise pertain to the current curriculum reform movement. Actually, hundreds of textbooks, teachers' manuals, films, brochures, and reports—too numerous to list here—produced by the several projects have supplied the basic data used in the foregoing descriptions and analyses.

There are many questions to be answered in curriculum planning, some of them close to the learner and some of them quite remote from him. The second group of readings sets forth some of these persistent questions as well as data sources that might profitably be consulted in trying to answer them. It should provide useful background for persons who think of curriculum as a course of studies.

More than the curriculum is undergoing change in American education. Proposals for reform include team teaching, nongraded schools, programed instruction, redesigned buildings and facilities, new approaches to teacher education, and so on. The third group of readings lists publications relevant to the broad-scale educational reform movement now under way.

I. The Current Curriculum Reform Movement

American Association for the Advancement of Science. *The New School Science*. Washington: The Association, 1963, pp. 92.

A collection of papers on the new science curricula, prepared for a series of nine regional conferences for school administrators.

American Council of Learned Societies and the National Council for the Social Studies. *The Social Studies and the Social Sciences*. New York: Harcourt, Brace & World, Inc., 1962, pp. 303.

Specialists in history, geography, political science, economics, cultural anthropology, sociology, and psychology, and in Asiatic, Russian, and Eastern European studies present the concepts, knowledge, and techniques contributed by their disciplines that are important for students to acquire by the end of their senior year in high school.

Association for Supervision and Curriculum Development. *Using Current Curriculum Development*. Washington: The Association, 1963, pp. 118.

A description of course development activity in most pre-collegiate fields; includes a list of projects, their sponsorship, headquarters' addresses, and materials produced through 1962.

College Entrance Examination Board. *The Challenge of Curricular Change*. New York: College Entrance Examination Board, 1966, pp. 151.

This collection of papers, presented at a colloquium co-sponsored by the CEEB and the National Association of Secondary-School Principals, both examines changes taking place in the high-school curriculum and discusses implications for colleges.

Educational Services Incorporated. *Goals for School Mathematics*. The Report of the Cambridge Conference on School Mathematics. Boston: Houghton Mifflin Co., 1963, pp. 102.

This report of twenty-nine scholars sets forth an outline of the mathematics that should and, it is believed, can be acquired in thirteen years of schooling; that is, in roughly the equivalent of three years of top-level college training today. Further, the report recommends that this kind of preparation—continuing through college and teacher training—take place today for those who will be teachers tomorrow.

116

Heath, Robert W. (ed.). *New Curricula*. New York: Harper and Row, 1964, pp. 292.

One of the few books that attempt to describe curriculum change in the academic subjects as well as to discuss some of the broader issues involved in the current reform; papers by Paul Woodring, Max Beberman, Jerrold R. Zacharias, Bentley Glass, Lee J. Cranbach, James R. Killian, Jr., Sterling M. McMurrin, and others.

National Council of Teachers of English. *The National Interest and the Teaching of English*. Chicago: The Council, 1961, pp. 140.

Deals with problems of improving teacher preparation, conditions under which teachers work (such as overload), and the lack of sequence in language, literature, and composition curricula.

National Elementary Principal, XLIII (September, 1963), pp. 92.

A collection of articles on changes in mathematics, science, social studies, language arts, and foreign languages in elementary schools, with supporting papers on the role of innovations, the allotment of time, and technological changes.

Project on the Instructional Program of the Public Schools. *The Scholars Look at the Schools*. A Report of the Disciplines Seminar. Washington: National Education Association, 1962, pp. 63.

Specialists in most of the academic disciplines set forth their views on how their fields should be reformed and included in the pre-collegiate curriculum.

School Review, 70 (Spring, 1962), pp. 147.

An entire issue on biology, chemistry, physics, mathematics, and testing in the new curriculum programs, including articles on the role of the National Science Foundation and on certain effects of current curriculum planning.

Social Education, XXIX (April, 1965), XXIX (November, 1965).

These issues present brief reports from a number of centers of the Social Studies Program. The April issue lists the new centers established in 1964, and concludes with the journal's annual review of curriculum materials. Its opening article provides a progress report on the program as a whole.

II. Curriculum Theory and Practice

Association for Supervision and Curriculum Development. *New Insights and the Curriculum*. Washington: The Association, 1963, pp. 328.

An attempt to show the implications of certain views of human potentiality, knowledge, social interaction, cultural values and valuing, citizenship, and creativity for curriculum planning.

Bloom, Benjamin S. (ed.). *Taxonomy of Educational Objectives: Cognitive Domain*. New York: Longmans, Green and Co., 1956, pp. 207.

Although published ten years ago, this book (with its companion volume, "the Affective Domain," see below) must be regarded as the standard guide to the clarification and evaluation of objectives at all levels of education. Despite its importance, it seems to have escaped the attention of most curriculum builders.

Elam, Stanley (ed.). *Education and the Structure of Knowledge*. Fifth Annual Phi Delta Kappa Symposium on Educational Research. Chicago: Rand McNally and Co., 1964, pp. 277.

Eight papers set forth not only the aspects of structure in the basic realms of knowledge but also some of the problems and issues to be taken into account in dealing with structure in the curriculum. Opening and concluding papers by Joseph J. Schwab and Arno A. Bellback, respectively, provide the broader perspective.

Ford, G. W. and Pugno, Lawrence (eds.). *The Structure of Knowledge and the Curriculum*. Chicago: Rand McNally and Co., 1964, pp. 105.

Again, a theme-setting paper by Schwab (see above), this time with four treatises on the structure of the natural sciences, mathematics, English, and the social studies.

Herrick, Virgil E. *Strategies of Curriculum Development* (edited by James B. Macdonald, Dan W. Anderson, and Frank B. May). Columbus, Ohio: Charles C. Merrill Books, Inc., 1965, pp. 196.

A collection of papers from the works of the late Virgil Herrick who devoted a considerable portion of his career to matters of curriculum theory. His discussion of curriculum design, little treated in the literature, is particularly noteworthy and relevant to current curriculum reform.

King, Arthur R., Jr., and Brownell, John A. *The Curriculum and the Disciplines of Knowledge*. New York: John Wiley and Sons, 1966, pp. 221.

"A theory of the curriculum which affirms the centrality of the communities of discourse" and a discussion of the problems for which such a theory has relevance.

Krathwohl, David R., Bloom, Benjamin S., and Masia, Bertram B. *Taxonomy of Educational Objectives: Affective Domain*. New York: David McKay Co., 1964, pp. 196.

The companion piece to the handbook on the cognitive domain (see above). No work similar to these two taxonomies but dealing with the psychomotor realm of behavior (and educational objectives) is as yet available.

Mager, Robert F. *Preparing Objectives for Programed Instruction*. San Francisco: Fearon Publishers, 1962, pp. 62.

A programed, "how-to-do-it" handbook for learning how to state educational objectives behaviorally.

Schwab, Joseph J., and Brandwein, Paul F. *The Teaching of Science*. The Inglis and Burton Lectures for 1961. Cambridge, Mass.: Harvard University Press, 1962, pp. 152.

Two essays that contain suggestions for sound curriculum organization and good teaching in virtually any field.

Smith, B. Othanel, and Ennis, Robert H. (eds.). *Language and Concepts in Education*. Chicago: Rand, McNally and Co., 1961, pp. 221.

Thirteen essays with analyses of problems and issues important in curriculum planning and teaching.

Tyler, Ralph W. *Basic Principles of Curriculum and Instruction*. Chicago: University of Chicago Press, 1950, pp. 83.

The primer for curriculum planners in any educational enterprise; specifies some basic questions and suggests where some of the answers may be found.

III. The Educational Reform Movement

Brown, B. Frank. *The Nongraded High School*. Englewood Cliffs, N. J.: Prentice-Hall, Inc., 1963, pp. 223.

An account of individualizing student progress in a Florida high school, a program that includes nongrading, independent study, "throw-away" report cards, and a host of other innovations.

Bruner, Jerome S. *The Process of Education*. Cambridge, Mass.: Harvard University Press, 1960, pp. 97.

One of the most quoted statements of faith in the ability of children to learn any subject in an intellectually honest form at any age.

Conant, James B. *The Education of American Teachers*. New York: McGraw-Hill Book Co., 1963, pp. 275.

A carefully documented analysis of problems and issues in educating teachers for elementary and secondary schools, with recommendations for curricula, certification, accreditation, employment, and in-service education.

Conant, James B. *Shaping Educational Policy*. New York: McGraw-Hill Book Co., 1964, pp. 139.

This may well prove to be the most influential of Conant's several reports on the condition of American education in that it sets forth the idea and the guidelines for creating the Compact for Education accepted in 1966 by thirty-three states and three territories of the United States. The Education Commission of the States is now a functioning reality.

Cremin, Lawrence A. *The Genius of American Education*. Horace Mann Lecture. Pittsburgh Press, 1965, pp. 122.

This provocative little book comments on curricula in addition to those of the schools and addresses itself to the question of what knowledge is of most value.

Cremin, Lawrence A. *The Transformation of the Schools*. New York: Alfred A. Knopf, 1961, pp. 387.

In part, an analysis of curricular influences prior to 1957; a knowledge of these developments is necessary to place the current movement in social perspective.

Evans, Luther, and Arnstein, George E. (eds.). *Automation and the Challenge to Education*. Proceedings of a symposium sponsored by the Project on the Educational Implications of Automation. Washington: National Education Association, 1962, pp. 190.

Specialists view the far-reaching implications of automation for the instructional as well as management aspects of education.

Goodlad, John I., and Anderson, Robert H. *The Nongraded Elementary School*. Revised edition. New York: Harcourt, Brace & World, Inc., 1963, pp. 248.

A proposal for reorganizing the school, in part to accommodate a curriculum organized vertically around fundamental concepts, principles, and modes of inquiry.

Goodlad, John I., O'Toole, John F., Jr., and Tyler, Louise L. *Computers and Information Services in Education*. New York: Harcourt, Brace & World, Inc., 1966, pp. 165.

A survey of current computer use in education, a report on promising practices, and some comments on the depressing state-of-the-art in schools as compared with industry and the military.

Keppel, Francis. *The Necessary Revolution in American Education*. New York: Harper and Row, 1966, pp. 201.

Deals with most of the larger questions pertaining to education for all and current inequalities therein, shaping state and national educational policy, educating teachers, and planning the curriculum. Keppel's personal commitment to education and to educational leadership is noticeable throughout.

National Society for the Study of Education. *The Changing American School*. Sixty-Fifth Yearbook of the National Society for the Study of Education. Chicago: University of Chicago Press, 1966, pp. 319.

A first section, describing some of the major changes in the schools since World War II and what is thought to have caused them, is followed by a second on forces and ideas to which the schools should have been responding during this last quarter century.

Project on Instruction. *Schools for the Sixties*. A Report of the National Education Association Project on Instruction. New York: McGraw-Hill Book Co., 1963, pp. 146.

The summary volume of an NEA effort to speak for the teaching profession on vital curricular and instructional issues.

Project on the Instructional Program of the Public Schools. *Deciding What to Teach* (written by Dorothy M. Fraser). Washington: National Education Association, 1963, pp. 264.

Examines the problems of deciding what to include in the curriculum and lists a series of recommendations for dealing with them.

Project on the Instructional Program of the Public Schools. *Planning and Organizing for Teaching* (written by John I. Goodlad). Washington: National Education Association, 1963, pp. 190.

Examines and defends alternative proposals for organizing school, curriculum, classroom, and instructional resources in American education.

Shaplin, Judson T., and Olds, Henry F. (eds.). *Team Teaching*. New York: Harper and Row, 1964, pp. 430.

A comprehensive treatment of the theory and practice of team teaching based primarily on the experience of faculty members at Harvard's Graduate School of Education with cooperating schools in the region.

Stoddard, George D. *The Dual Progress Plan*. New York: Harper and Row, 1961, pp. 225.

A translation of the cultural duality concept into curricular and organizational duality in the elementary school.